Inherit the Blood

poetry & fiction by

Barney Bush

Thunder's Mouth Press
New York   Chicago

Published in the United States by Thunder's Mouth Press, Box 780, New York, NY 10025 and Box 11223, Chicago, IL 60611

Design by L. Bolchert

Funded in part by grants from the New York State Council on the Arts and the National Endowment for the Arts.

Some of the poems in this book have appeared in the following publications:

The Madison Review, University of Wisconsin;
Pudding, The Ohio Poetry Therapy Center and Library;
New Letters, The University of Missouri, Kansas City;
High Rock Review, Saratoga Springs, New York;
Visions, Black Buzzard Press, Arlington, VA;
Blind Alleys, 7th Son Press, Baltimore, MD
and one poem from each of the following books by Barney Bush

Petroglyphs, The Greenfield Review Press;
My Horse And A Jukebox, UCLA through Native American Studies;
Longhouse of The Blackberry Moon, Ethnic Studies, New Mexico Highlands University, Las Vegas;

Thanks to The National Endowment for The Arts for their support and to the following: PEN American Center, Author's Guild Fund, Daryl Trivieri, and to Jeanne Blum.

Library of Congress Cataloging in Publication Data

Bush, Barney.
    Inherit the blood.

    1. Indians of North America—Poetry.   I. Title:
Inherit the blood.   II. Title: Abbey of the bear.
PS3552.U8162I5   1985   811'.54   84-24052
ISBN 0-938410-28-8 (pbk.)

Distributed by:
Persea Books
225 Lafayette St.
New York NY 10012
(212) 431-5270

Prologue

Traditional people, in the positive sense, are ones who seek power to secure their relationship with all of creation, to accommodate faithfully the Giver of Life, and for maintaining alertness to ever changing balances in accommodation's ceremonies.

There is an intrinsic balance in all nature; mankind's quest for wealth, and power over other human lives is the chief upset in this delicate, albeit firm, rule. Any form of service to greed is inconsistent with our Creator's universe. . . . when one becomes addicted, the ceremonies fail; motion and prayer become disparate, and therefore, the spirit of mankind.

We, the native peoples of this world, are the ultimate victims of this unholy power, and through oppression, become its willing participants. A native person is anyone who is from this earth and does not seek power over the lives of others. Anthropologists will, of course, point out inter-tribal warfare as contradiction to the latter statement. This is understandable as most anthropologists, at least in this portion of the world, are also victims of this colonist government that is a mere two hundred years old, and yet influenced by its recent and barbaric entry into our world. We who surrender are at fault. To continually blame our oppressors for our weaknesses is folly, and self-defeating. In surrendering, we give approval to the children, while creating traditions that give ceremony to humanity's darkest side.

Vision must be constantly guarded and renewed; assuredly by those who have remained devoted to the lives designed by our Creator, and by those who seek the strength to return to the love of what is right. And to you who seek, to you who imagine you have lost the will to seek, to those who seek allies with whom to share your newly awakened strength, and to those possessed, who continue the barbarity, this book is designed and written for your many names.

May it be so.

Fred Peters Floyd

1939–1983

Bernie Morning Gun

1950's–1984

Larry Red Shirt

1950–1983

Margaret Richmond

1921–1982

Merceline Sanapaw

1914–1984

Abram Track

1952–1984

Donald (Bud) Ward

1944–1984

Pahoo Dan

1960–1983

Last nights moon   opened
power of seeds   rich earth
Ohio and Mississippi River
villages bring forth the
sacred objects
On flat topped mounds   wise
elders confer   bless the
seeds in moonlight
Moons power   songs of our
elders   are handsome male
and female spirit
Wet bottomlands   thick with
budding limbs   night peepers
crickets   wind of rushing
water   stir with morning
sun   grandfather the
nourisher   the mid husband for
children about to be born

Greedy Ones   as you leave
take your sacred icons
statue of liberty   nuclear
cores   draglines   cancer
the gold in Ft Knox   take
your names with you   to
your world beyond the stars
and   with madlike laughter
know your manifest destiny is
not complete   until each
planet bears your flag

i remember wind   i remember
last nights moon   songs in
the circle of my silhouette
i remember etching these
symbols onto this
conch shell disk   i
remember the origin of our
world   what foreigners in
forty years will scientifically
say is   inherited in the
blood.

Inside the star
inside the holy circle
firelight shadows dance on
faces awaiting word   somewhere
spinning time in the prairie wind
listening for prayers to make
their way

It must be well   with
good tobacco   good heart toward
all beings
the sun   the sky   all that
inhabit there and on earth   for
in the stars emblazoned image is
power   sacred hearts blood
flowing through the veins of
earth

Eyes recount every movement
An unadorned warrior wears only the
white plume from under the eagles tail
Long white blacktipped feathers are
voices of the people
Seeing improperly will lose one in
dark dreams that will come back
forever.

Over northeast mountains
blue bellied clouds weld
into opalescence
Early morning wind came from
my sleep   southwest
vision where herbs
hang from vigas   drying
And paint dries on canvas
stretched by moons
reflection in
last nights creek
Bare feet quietly pace
the east window to the
west   streaking
brown eyes with new color
new light   glaring from
the brush tip   trapped
inside the voyeurs green
mirrors   feigning
sleep   longing for
bare feets torso   and
brown eyes   to inch its
way back here   beneath
this warm starquilt.

Shimmering in worlds that
stay in the blood
worlds where there is
no room   removed from
memory   until there is
need
Wind will cry through
trees   through
the mothers mouth   who
must sweat   grunt   until
the new season slips out
like a new buffalo calf
covered with sweat   and
blood   like the
crying of a nation whose
time has returned.

They say Cain was marked
Many of europes descendants
who preach their blend of
Christianity say Cain was
marked black   a
punishment for his violent
crime that all might know
him and his heirs
Brown male and female
children and elders   whose
heads   whose hands   whose
vaginas and genitals did
not appear as trophies on
poles in Boston Square   on
hats and saddles of generals
or on walls of settlers
cabins   brown male and
female who were not shipped
as slaves to far off lands
who did not die of syphilis
or smallpox   who   filled
with laced rum   did not
kill each other or sell
their wives and children
these ones who did not kill
themselves in remote prisons
or freeze or starve to death
on removal trails and retreats
these few that in desperation
fell to knees praying to
blackrobed gods
these ones of us left standing
light brown to dark
know   that   IN THE BEGINNING
not one was
created white.

When i have not seen brothers
a long time
when i have not seen sisters
a long time
when we have not seen each
other for a long time
we look deeply into our
dreams   the ones that have
caused this to be so
Songs   mountains   prairies
drums   relatives   bear
elk   turtle   eagle and
we see it is so
Embracing is the dreams
roundness
In the blood   the journey
never ends.

The Most Beautiful Side of Ourselves Is Our Love for Our Homes—the Ugliest Side Is in the Desperation of Defending Our Homeland from Those Who Destroy It

Beware   earth destroyers
You have stolen   stripped
sold   bought   stolen the
land you could have lived on
in peace
All prices are paid
Creator   give us strength
to surrender our vengeance
our sorrow   so that
you may accept it as pity on
all of us   and
return to us wearing the
plume from under the eagles
tail   so that
your children may recognize
you
Earth destroyers do not
recognize eagles plumes
do not know that the
earth will turn
upon them.

On this bluff   glowing
white moon makes grandmothers
country real again
Saplings below turn their
leaves as if stars settle
among them
Smokey moisture in valleys
valleys   that know our
blood   know what
blood does
i can hear their voice
behind blue haze
katydids   cicadas
owls voice bouncing from
stone walls
Their songs pull as if my
cord has not been cut   and
everything will be
new again   even my
grandmothers dress   sewn
with strong sinew
With this flute   this
light   i can almost smell
her   In this light the
moon becomes the concha on
her belt.

In the Sweat Lodge

The door is sealed
Sightless black but for
embers of cedar and
sweetgrass   sprinkled
on fiery stones
Shuffling next to sweated
flesh   i cough   prepare
my heart for prayer
Outside   corn is ripe
gardens heavy
It is the last night before
cut hair
Dogs are restless like the
hazy sky that has chilled
air in mid august
Our relatives move stoically
knowingly   tasks to finish
before morning   move by
instinct like the river of
birds in fall
Rain comes late   fiercely
turns late summers leaves
upside down   cools the
sizzling earth   summers
swelter before it is finished
cools the whitemans locust
energy at the edge of Yellowstone
where grizzlies catch their
last breath   muddies
creeks   bottoms in southern
illinois where stripminers
gleefully waste another ten
thousand acres   cools
radioactive eyes
One night left before the
sunrise of Grandmothers death
Her stories are all around me

can feel all our relatives blood
all those stories entrusted to
me   to grandchildren who
may never to this life be born
Without our world   i look
across to where our relatives
dance   on land that is clean
forever   where europes brands
that worship goldthirsty gods
are myths
It is only a wind   i hear
them say.

Written for Johhny Kiro When I Heard in March 1978 That He Had Drowned in an August Lake Somewhere Out East of Gallup

My eyes always look far
away
with dogs that stare off
to distant movements
Oklahoma summer rains
cover me   Colorado
snows have held me bound
until i could once
more see the horizon
Dance for me   he said
lighting his tobacco

Are those antelope in the
field   They will dance
for you

Soon elk come through
the valleys   seeking
the new grass
Johnny the Laguna stalks
them
people will be coming
home
My eyes look to see them. . . . . .

Who Listens for the Children
for Pat Locke
Flying Earth

Who hears these songs that
bond to life   for
which English has no words
these songs that will turn
that power around
Those who hear   who
seek to hear
for the children
for this earth
must fast   must
seek the power that is
dormant   unconscious
It is a warriors road
There is nothing on this
road to help us that europe
has brought   Listen
The power that possesses
them   has made cataracts
over human eyes   and
causes children to turn
guns upon themselves
Who hears these songs
sung by isolated warriors
who pray   burn
their cedar on silent
hillsides   asking
for the power to reach
our hearts
Pray for those who sing
who seek freedom   who
seek other warriors   who
seek peace in our homeland
Pray for our anger   that
it does not blind us

Pray for the whitepeople
whose blindness   whose
chemicals choke roots in
the soil   suffocate
water beings   suffocates
humans   whose blindness
promises nuclear winters and
death throughout the earth
Who listens while we yet
pretend to be alive?

Blood

for Richard Emerson
Jack

Turning deer flesh over
the hot fire   turning
my face from the oak
smoke   i smelled you
You are almost here
          Ahneen Neegi
Where do you sit tonight
i am smiling for you
Coyotes wail at bottom of
the bluff   and here a
sacred glow   my own blood
where there are
blessings in every wind
In the fire   my
transfixed eyes flicker
inviolably   wanting to
see you in the gentle
light   holy way in our
blood   terrestrial blood
our way that others presume
The meat is roasted   blood
to be devoured by humid
summer breezes or
winds that bite with
teeth of winter ice.

for Aunt Roxie

Her body is old   her joy
is sixteen   but hair like
sycamore in winter sky
It is summer   Humidity
clings to blackberry briars
to our furrowed brows that
scan the hilltop for
graves whose names are inscribed
only in her mind   graves
yet unencumbered by americas
highways   yet secure from
graverobbers shovels
i look upon this hill of
encased ancestors   fit in
their presence to stories of
scrambled retreats before the
locusts of red   white and blue
In the eyes of my aunt   who
knows the entombed only through
stories   they are last falls
burials
She repeats the stories to us
who stay beside her
looks deeply into my veins and
speaks with the voice of those
who carved marble effigys   This
is the last time I will come here

It was the first time for me   and
for my son who picks near ripe
berries with his uncle and
grandmother at the edge of
the forest.

Silent Witness
for Bud
Spring '84

It was last nights moon
that brought   the
sound   voices in the
creek   erupting in
nights reflections
dissolving in spring
runoff   as that
ancestral moon of ours
that round glowing face
that has viewed all of
nighttimes history
stared into my own   She
is our grandmother   but
i cry out to one who sees
through day and night
and to you who begins the
last distance of the sacred
journey   you who has
left this awesome distance
these memories of when we
were first walking upright
hurling razor edged knives
to the boundaries of human
flesh   spread eagled to
the barn   and plotted
sinister hoaxes at community
rituals   Even in
sunlit forest journeys
swimming holes   there were
desperate retreats on horses
backs   and
that first time below humid
ancients grounds   at
the creekbank door   within

the circle of sunlight
where birds grew silent on
limbs   salty beads
erupted from brown pores
stinging the eyes   the
lips
It was a ceremony   ours
as we shared the blood
Below the hill of ancient ones
whose silence was broken by
the pounding of our hearts
we could smell the damp
broken soil   a spring wind
that almost wailed   almost
mourned for us   Sometimes
i still wake whispering your
name.

Long sunburnt hair matted to
sweat on his cheeks   He was
yet walking at summers edge
still going home somewhere
before winter set in
It was america   but he was
not an american though born in
blood of this earth
Prisons were everywhere
In them he had seen his face a
thousand times over   seen
headless bones of ancestors
scattered over hillsides   over
stripmine dumps   left by
looters who sell even the
fleshless skulls
In sprawl of urban bars
blueblack   fleshfilled   nights
stirred with razor edges
used on his own blood
Short term prison for killing
one of his own   even though
he pretended they were white
He woke up that last morning
lips puffed   slivers of
glass in his teeth   hands
too unsteady to grasp the
tiny thorns of the beer bottle
Gazing at the faceless body
lying next to him   wondering
if he had been kissing on it
he laughed at himself
Survival was still with him
even more   when he sees bodies
of those who lost it   for
whom dreams were not enough
nor religion held together by

witchcraft and white gods   or
elders who sip their bottles
beside the drum
As he walks   he shakes his
head   at whites who call earth
a savage wilderness   and their
cities   civilization   whose
infertile bodies   infertile
minds   steal   adopt native
children   send them to mental
institutions   when they cannot
imitate   when they cannot
turn from their blood
His head shakes until he feels
his brains ready to explode
when he hears white leaders
condemning atrocities   pleading
for humanity   with ears and
hearts closed when his own make
the same pleas to americas
leaders
He stares at the golden rods and
sweet william   grandparents
memory somehow attached   searches
back to when stone was made
smooth to fit the hand
It is enough   he thinks
holding round stone from
Old Town in his palm
pinches out a bit of ancient
tobacco
Hot   hazy sky clouds with
autumn wind   Balsam limbs
whine   Shadowy figures
circle the white drum   sing
in presence of White Plumed
Spirit   seen by ones

created from this earth
He walks   listens for
voices of relatives   listens for
songs   listens for
thundering of hooves   listens for
wailing behind prison walls
wailing of power hungry spirits
spilling from carcasses of newly
born
He listens until he hears cracking
of silence   smells the
bowels of earth   and
downpour of rain causes the bear to
stand upright.

It Is Finished

The dreams are old before you
say them   round around
round   and
moons silent figure attracts
your whisper
Humanitys dark bell thunders
loudly   in bellies that
hunger for war
i sit here with you in this
dream   this photograph among
my mothers sons   this
campsmoke
this moment   another time
already lived
What crying night wind do
your soulful eyes release
like an invisible lariat to
hold me at a manitos edge
When we are alone   alone
our words are cedar boughs
bending   but my
Shawnee voice cracks   when
we divide
Within the circle we
sing   harmony revolving
in all directions   like
the spirit of blue light that
pours from our mouths
spirit within spirit   once
broken from the circle
wanders aimlessly   until
we dream
dreams inside dreams.

Directions in Our Blood
for two suns
Phil and Colin

I

West Kansas full moon
cool breeze   leads us
through heat that killed
60 people in St Louis
this same moon that made
light for families on
horseback   travois and
hardtimes journeying into
this buffalo country
Crickets   cicadas   dance
inside my road weary
head   We watch the
night   and grassy plains
i tell my two sons who
want to sit on every hill
that every shadow is a
buffalo spirit   They
watch from the truck bed
and watch me too   marking
with my eyes   roads on
which their mothers and i
have hitchhiked   And
there is a road filled
with summer moons   where
a hitchhikers nostrils
bleed from stings of
winter stars   years ago
even now   the road smells
the same
When i am moving   when
we are moving   there is
an urgency like escaping a
world surrounded by wagon

trains   sometimes like
escaping with their horses
Morning   Nights prairie
filled with buffalo and
covered with grass   has
been plowed under   replaced
with urban sprawl
with miles of electric and
telephone wires   My sons
shut their eyes to sleep
through it   to wake up
from this dream   i pull
over to wake up too

II

One week in Boulder at
Charlies   (the original
Navajo taco himself)
in his two pueblo sized
rooms   that are crammed
with files   proposals and
government resolutions that
date back to the first
Long Walk starring Kit Carson
a cast of Navajo patriots
some sheep and silver bridles
In Boulder my two boys burn
out on white girls   video
games   movies and roller
skates   burning down to
the excitement of freedom
from vermont mentality
burning on the taste of
roads in their blood
They say   Lets go   and
i say   Load up the truck
We cross mountains to

Lindas hogan   to her
mansion of wild herbs and
grasses   her daughters
luminous eyes that shine
like two polished apache
tears   Linda takes
me out   now get this   to
the loudest cowboy bars in
colorado   where she dances
with every cowboy but me
Hell   i just shoot pool
with her rejects   consoling
some   Yes i think she is
always like this   and
i like pool better than
dancing anyway   Thats what
he said
My boys are loaded up again
Got me ready just in time
to drive past the sundown
and they wrestle all the
way over Wolf Creek Pass
all the way to Ignacio   right
into the front door of my
cousins house

III

Being with relatives is
always a long story   where
time is long hours
long afternoons doing
beadwork   stringing chokers
sewing moccasins   some for
gas money to get to powwows on
If you are indian   you will
understand about my relatives
Hanko is really my brother

but i call him my cousin because
he belongs to a different
tribe   and his cheekbones
are a little higher too   his
rear ones
At breakfast   one of the
meals between morning and noon
Hanko asks my boy Colin if
he has ever been with a woman
Colin says   Well   uh   sort
of like   well
Hanko says to my other boy
Phil   have you ever been with
a woman   Phil says yes
Hanko says   Now see Colin   all
you have to say is yes or no
Colin says no
Hanko says   OK   I just wanted
to know
Ball games are played at night
on every res in n america
Big white lights stare down
into brown faces   scattered
about the diamond   reminding
me of BIA training films
My boys skirt the perimeter
fighting off mosquitoes and
looking for women
The rest of us sit in back
of pickup trucks   watching
sometimes yelling   but mostly
watching   sometimes laughing
sometimes recalling old memories
The same cars drive round and
round   same eyes checking us
out   We check back   sometimes
wave   but mostly we
watch

IV

Between Pagosa Springs and
Chama NM   a wedge from
another world   Out past
Red Ryders Rodeo grounds is
the road through the yellow
veil   a world that whitemen
have left partially intact
a road almost too sacred to
mention
My boys ride in the back
sitting high   their faces
prowing through this artery
        liquid mesas
        summer aspen
sweet smell of pine air
Hitchhiker   waistdeep in
roadside grass   a short
haired whiteman who makes up
songs for indians
He sings one for us   We
tell him that   Brave Buck
is not really a good name
for a indian song   He is
willing to learn   We explain
and he can laugh   So can we
At Echo Canyon   one of
the old days stopovers for us
Ft Lewis students   we stop
again   midnight   cougar
tracks   We put out tobacco for
all the relatives   Every star
is watching   Once   i heard
the name of Jesus spoken
and it is here that i realize
instructions given to whitemen

on how to live on this earth
have never been taken   and
it is here that i hear how the
doors to their heaven have
been shut against them   and
it is here that i finally
understand why the whiteman
behaves savagely   and there
is more but another time
My son Phil is eager to see
his mother   We hear
her silver bracelets
clanging   rhythmically   like
her laughter   Her door light
pyramids into the darkness

V

On the straight away east
out of a New Mexico sundown
my two sons   full of
adrenelin and sopapillas
rock the truckbed   until
i am swerving all over the
road
They get up front   with
me   wrestle open skies and
massive clouds retreating
behind the rainbow
My boys wrestle into oncoming
headlights and signs that say
Oklahoma City   349 miles
Through rainstorms passing on
to northwest mountains   we
blaze into the cool shadows
of   truck driving nights
bearing down on the plains
into the Texas Panhandle and

on to Oklahoma
The long road of old 66 is
americas last rough edge of
the automobile age
Alongside is highway 40
smoothing out americas land
scape   smoothing out the
kinks in manifest destiny
but yet we ride   through
herds of buffalo that by day
are stands of mesquite and
juniper
Our headlights search out
bug infested humid air   the
road to my brothers
No lights in the house but
our headlights bounce off
greasy looking faces   slick
hair and aluminum cans
They said they had been waiting
that someone was coming
We are here   silence   We
touch each others faces and
remember the smells   Children
come from sleep   Chris   Jon
Phil   Colin   We cannot see
blood shot eyes   cannot see
all the beauty   even with
dawn about to break

VI

My pickup is a lathered
roan   kicking red dust
from Calumet OK onto the
Will Rogers turnpike
blazing into eastern hills
blazing through the

history of native nations
with political turmoil   and
defense   somehow linked to
savagery   written in
white texts   whose
realities are undeveloped
but whose destruction nears
perfection   We carry
their symbols in our
ceremonies   i say i
am your kin   your blood
but my source is further
east   from these Oklahoma
hollers   Every trail i
take is one of tears   and
the return is no less
severe than the exodus
On 60 East out of Spring
field   MO   heading for the
homeland   nights aroma
already cooling into dreams
Midnight riders are the
truck stop cowboys slicing
Ozark air past me   and
my kids in the travois bed
We ride night like invisible
spectres   at the edge of
frontier settlements
i sing   pull in at quiet
one light gas stops
White traveler who sees our
blood   nods a mystic
gesture   sympathetic but
longing reverence for our
crimson past   i teach my
boys to nod back   to keep
the song that is being sung

inside   keep it going a
little longer   to let them
know that no one sees the
other side without a song.

No drums   no songs rolling
over plains   along river banks
a lonesome land without song
without human beings
Coyote pauses
Coyote cries out   in mime
Without song   coyote is
lonesome too
Rivers yet tumult   spring
thaws   warm summer rain
sinks deeply into soil   into
fleshless jaws rigidly open
from the last song
Millions of birth places   once
fond musing in hearts of
mothers   fathers   children
once even holy thoughts
places with secret names   long
forgotten   evaporated into
silence   like a dream traveling
without wind   a dream that
flies over canyon rims
down between sandstone walls
like a breath with no
lips   no sound
a dream that never reached in
time   to a sleeping being
Even the clear blue water is
as silent as it is deep
The dream yet moves
pauses   to listen
      coyote
Coyote has found blood
Coyote shrills like a
newborn baby.

Voice in the Blood

Outside
yellow leaves rattle
My eyes squint between
realities   all those
relatives in my
dreams   and fields of
dark antlered clouds
rationing sunlight into
shadows beside my bed
Wind sounds like it
should be cold   like
there should be geese
the ones who snatched
up my great grandmothers
ghost   that quiet
childhood time when i
was watching
i was alone with her
didnt know what i was
supposed to do to
stop them
Beneath her star blanket
she told me in words as
old as this earth   not
to listen
i told her it was too
late
She wanted to protect the
blood   the silence that
she left me   as she
went south over amber
hills
as grandmothers do every
fall   knowing they
have grandchildren   half
behind   half
with them.

I

Crouched on one knee   one
hand on the wet limestone
edge   he appeared ready to
leap   but it was wind
rain biting into his face
nights cold dark rain
dampening fall that has
begun to settle   His
childhood friends were
walking ghosts   calling
his name in the woods behind
him   descendants of
blood   stone axes rounded
grooves
Gusts of wind shaped like
luminous waves from the
great river   whistled
through his hair   his ears
                whistled
like short bursts from
flute   into memory that
weaves wet nights into a
billion years   His
eyes are the web.

II

He is the smell of wet
leaves   the smell like an
animals musk   that he
has left on cornerstones of
america
But here   forest is his
mothers teats   his
grandmother teats   his
wifes teats   nourishing

him and those to come
Sunlight melting into
scarlett limbs is his
grandfathers breath   all
that breathe it are brother
and sister
Among relatives   female
goes first through the door
Among enemies   male spirit
enters first
It is the way of this life.

III

Bare feet that left the
ledge before daylight
avert thorns   sharp
edges like a wildcats
paws
He is the seeker of
night hollows   where
there are waterfalls and
owls hunt   where
brothers and sisters are
called by their names
It is autumn
Shadows stretch across
the mountains   Skies
darken   thunder
Wildgeese sound like
children playing
He feels warm sweat of
horseback on his inner
thighs   and shadows
catch him   blend his
shivering lean form into
cold rain.

Purple rocks   fluorspar
cerebellum   inside our
maternal earth   To hold
one piece is medicine
flesh of relatives   ghosts
in long dresses gathering
falls last harvest
hickory nuts   hard corn
Wide butts bend in
fields picking the remains
dragging burlap bags
through kids   dogs
the silence of remote
bottomlands
Silence is always there
whether one speaks aloud or
trees fill with crows
Deer at the edge   as
does the silence   think
themselves invisible   even
when they hear the click of
the trigger
Men   old and young   as
invisible as the deer
bury the heart
Entrails move inside the
purple crystal   so that
deer will always believe in
their own power   always
come back   always
hear the drums   the
songs made for them
                    always
listening   for the
feet inside their skins.

This Song Again

River clay grey hangs over
early fall
Chilling wetness   settling
on balsam limbs causes my
shirtless torso to shiver
Herds of elk bristled through
dreams   brandishing damp
ivory branches   eyes surveying
frosted air snorting through
caverns of alert nostrils
Air is dewy musk like the
odor in my blankets   like
brisk New Mexico nights where
these blankets warmed two un
restrained bodies
Changing winds   what white
men can never take from us
wind our grandfathers
grandmothers observed freely
anxiety among birds tasting
directions   swirling
designs darkening the sky
We are that memory living in
blood of elk   withdrawing
from alien habits to keep
freedom alive
Standing in field of sweet
grass   i am blood
forest odors withdrawing to
roots
i move my head like the elk
making song in the midst of
beauty   We live in
song.

Hiso Kiniwa*

Wet earth   beneath guileless
feet   yet to learn concrete
trails   impetuously carry
him into wind of his blood
through the door   his
brothers and father   wind
burned faces
His mothers silence   like
woodstove smoke   fragrant
but stoked with turbid eyes
knowing our blood doused
hands had killed meat   had
left entrails on autumn
leaves
With each step   each move
ment she makes   he smells
old villages   Ohio River
mud   sound bodies   not
lost in history but waiting
for their return
In stone moss laden air
blood whispers like the
aroma of river caves   blue
hollows   and midnights that
run with wolves
Countless last songs have
been sung   with only lime
stone walls to hear   but
they say before ending
thousands take up the chorus.

*crossover

48

i couldnt wait to
tell you everything   wanting
to be silent
Steel gray hanging like
fringe on a buckskin
shirt   quilled with dark
blue   and skies lodge
trapped the smoke   fusing
land too wet for dogs to
bark
Forest rounds its
vestige of blood into
dormant wells among the
roots   Your voice
through long wires connected
with my own
We both knew it was going
to snow
that we carried distance from
our own tribes
our distance from each
other   in our breath
silent voices that cry each
others name while we
sleep
Wind arched its heavy
back over wires   over
sounds that began when we
were born.

American Journey: The White Mans Educational TV Approach To Freedom For All

Sometimes you win   whiteman
and i forget   it is you who
smiles when i am broken   whe
n i panic   thinking where
will i get money to pay rent
or phone bill   or my nation
al defense student loan
Sometimes you win   on tv and
i become angry watching the
educational channel
American Journey   a whitema
n retracing steps of de Tocq
ueville   concluding that
    Americas experiment with
    democrazy has been succe
    ssful
and last scenes are despair
in native Alaskan fishing vi
llages
Yes   whiteman   sometimes yo
u win   but we are yet here
on our native soil   all the
way to Tierra del Fuego
blood quickly seeping into e
arth   in democratic splendo
r   clearing way for your m
aster plan
We are still here   and some
times you win   even as you
bootlick black folks   for
their votes   promising the
m a place in paradise
Blacks win too as pockets fi
ll with ransom money to aid

50

you in destruction   you bre
athlessly pray
We are still here   with suc
cessful part natives running
stoically with stars and str
ipes in one eye   dislocatio
n in the other   Sometimes y
ou win and i become angry be
cause your destruction is pl
ugging into every household
on the planet   bringing fre
edom and fast food   You hyp
ocrites   Freedom and food
were already here   but you
were not the distributors   Y
ou know who was   You loom a
s a great shadow between ear
th and sun   When suns power
wans   you are there with gl
eam of gold painted gods   Yo
u are death   painting your
color onto faces of millions
death that lays waste to all
of nature   and you call our
great patriots   blood thirs
ty savages   and make outlaw
s out of your own people who
love children
Yes whiteman   sometimes yo
u win   gloat in your americ
an journey   allying with su
ccessful majorities   depic
ting drunken natives crawlin
g from beneath automobiles

Yes   you win   Native people
win too   win the competitio
n   the finish line   for th
e most suicidal on earth   an
d successful white writers a
dvise me to
     Avoid the Indian trip
     and just write poetry
Hoh Wah ******************

It is a morning
Sun breaks into autumn frost
There is a silence as if the
whiteman has come and gone
Our windows steam from boil
ing choke cherries and
coffee   This morning i
light cedar   pray that my
son who walks knowingly this
blood drenched earth   to
your school   will replace
your american journey with a
human one.

Whose Voice

My father taught
me the sound of
screech owl   Semyalwa
late fall evenings
when aroma of wood
smoke seared lungs and
watered eyes
He would peep around
trees at me   a
crazy face   making
owls sound   when
purple thistle and
golden rod altered the
skys vision   when
our land was
frosted shadows that
thawed stories of
grandparents
Semyalwas voice yet
startles me   where
the road breaks   when
i think i am
alone   and i will
still shiver.

Taking A Captive/1984
For Mike Gavlak

A light drizzle falling   off
and on for days
Kentucky hills   yellow leaves
matted to damp black   your
pensive eyes in smokey hollows
My son   you are born by
mistake in another world where
your vision lingers
too long
too long to teach those who
seek wisdom from the future
Three generations back   in
my village you would be
painted   have a name
Waylahskese
You would carry flute of
polished cedar   inlaid with
finest abalone shell   bound
with soft white buckskin
On humid evenings i would
hear your cavernous melodies
rolling off limestone bluffs
above Spaylawa Theepi
You would grow into manhood
bringing fresh meat to the
door of your grandmothers
weegiwa   carry
your opahwahka in the
oracle of your heart
Stalking figures yet roam
shadows of colonial america
yet drawing breath   continuous
memory absorbed into blood
Your ivoried tiger form spoors
its way to my heart   not as
a killer but as   one of grace

Here in my center   M'qua seeks
power to bring you home   sniffs
the air for winter
Too soon   Shemegana pepoou
Your real name awaits
Come into your dreams   my young
captive   hear the hawk shriek
as he soars outside your window
Come into the lodge of winter
dreams   hibernate with the
bear.

Spaylaway Theepi
Ohio River
Weegiwa
house
Opahwahka
Medicine
M'qua
Black bear
Shemegana pepoou
Foreign cold, threat of winter

55

You have come like a
shadow   riding the
whistle that dogs hear on
dusty roads
Wind you hear has been
inside me   blue storm
looming in   making each
movement   reawakening
Crows are laughing because
autumn has been brief   We
are from the same earth
fathered by the same silence
that has caused leaves to
fall
Face   turning to sunlight
silhouetting canyon shadows
you have brought
winter night   sound of
flute traveling in crystals
hooftracks frozen in stars of
winter lightening
Your boots sit inside my
door   long shadows jump
with flames against logs
Talk is long trails into
night hearts   speaking with
eyes lonesome for each other
Spruces bend beside the
window   whine in weariness
over aching minds   turned
blind   to November wind and
tobacco smoked skies
Northern Mystery has come to
its holy place   lying
long warm naked beneath
heavy blankets   hearing his
medicine song   feeling nights

bluesnow make smiles on
his face
Limbs scratch at the window of
childhood dreams   like
coyote songs on mountain ice
This euphony we sleep   by
morning is gone.

Southwind murmurs perceptably
through tall northern firs that
pierce skys darkness
The party was the same   the
same alcohol inspired laughter
His women love him better that
way
This night   full sensuous
lips   arc downward on his
slick brown face   no guttural
teasing   no aieeees from his
throat
His eyes glance off   into the
umbra of the forest
Under wild hair   southwinds
voice chills his ears   with
stories of what alcohol does
to earths native people
No one notices his footsteps
walking away   through
silhouettes of laughter   and
loneliness
He wanders door to door on the
res   looking for that face
the one that shares the voice
but in screen doors   yellow
light   faces solemnly offer
sandwiches or a place to sleep
as they have since the first
kegs came to this land
He eats   goes on   his
composure saturated with booze
and uppers
He knows and call their power
by names   wanders into light
before dawn   but he does not
forget   cannot forget   voice
that lingers in the southwind.

i angle my head
toward the moon
toward the stars
toward late winters
sky
not even a dogs bark
not even your warm
cheek brushing my
face   but the
dreams keep us
together
keep me wondering on
this short stretch of
the journey   which
one is the dream
Which season is our
dance   our road to
the shining water
where bowls are made of
river clay
Into this northeast night
my cedared frame angles
toward the moon.

Abbey of the Bear
for Ursule Molinaro with much affection

Hard years in Euroamerica's alien world have brought
Omar back to the headwaters of White Bird Creek. Child-
hood familiarity blends with his stagnant odor, sloshes
over mirrored rocks that dissolve the forest edge, spills
into the canyon's decaying wetness. The flood pours into
the bell of Omar's worlds. His body is almost six feet of
naked summer, hardened with prison tattoos, sheened in
Oklahoma humidity. Omar is a veteran . . . not of the
Viet Nam War that has just ended . . . but of the streets.
A squinting icon in the afternoon sun, he feels the rapid
beating of his heart, the rupturing of honky-tonk nights
that dull his memory. He steps reverently into the cool
river, kneads the sandy bottom with his toes, senses the
blue hill water edging up his calves. He scoops the liquid,

allows it to pour between his fingers, swallows it like whiskey of which there was never enough. His scream shatters the wall of cedar and black oak air as he abandons himself into the depths of White Bird Creek.

Around the corner of the log house, she carries her willow basket filled with plump blackberries and dewberries that she has picked from hillside briars. Old Annie possesses acute eyes that jet from side to side inside a face that bears the plum's lot of remaining in the sun too long. On summer mornings before the red sun devours the smokey mist, she wanders the dank hollows, harvesting plants and singing prayers. It is the whites who call her Old Annie. Among older native people, she is known as Gonawah Hequawi, Rainbow Woman. Many young people in the district call her Nohkohmis, Grandmother, as it is her leathered hands that pulled their mucoused bodies into this world. And this she is, by blood, to Omar. With bears and rainbows she exchanges secrets of earth and sky, of the spirit world and of the plants that reveal themselves to her. During winter nights elders tell stories of the times when the Southwind People first lived along the Spaylaway Theepi, Ohio River, and of the brave men and women who fought and died resisting the Greedy Ones. How diseases, alcohol, and murders of children and elders had destroyed their respect for the Greedy Ones as human beings. But the favorite story is told by hunters who have seen Old Annie conversing with P'qway, a gigantic female black bear, who lives somewhere in the bluffs above White Bird Creek. Eyes of children widen and sparkle when they hear that black bears used to be human beings.

Setting her basket down by the well, Annie sinks the bucket with one twisting jerk, distorting her shimmering image into whirlpools of darkness. She pours the entire contents through her harvest. The berries glitter like tiny clumps of midnight sky. This pleases her even though her eyes are fixed with concern, squinting perhaps more from the sunlight than the visit yesterday. Attorneys representing the Ozark Mining Company had approached her about testing her land for coal. She straightens her back and ponders over her garden patch. The corn is doing good. She wonders why she had heard Semyalwa, the owl, hooting down by the creek this morning. Hesitating on her weathered porch, she looks across the garden to the hills beyond. Some few berries roll from her basket as she turns, allowing the screen door to slam behind her.

He is near the valley and can hear cicadas humming their familiar way, familiar time of midsummer when it's even too hot to snag. The rolling meadows of his boyhood unfold before him. It is a land not too unlike the Ohio Valley of his grandparents. This was the final removal area, the last land that the Greedy Ones didn't want. And those who had not hidden in remote pockets of the east had come to call it home. To the west, the tribes who had followed the buffalo were settled on the open plains. Omar touches gently the large white pine under which he used to sit. There were always aunts and uncles and kids around the house of his nohkohmis. He remembers his mother always leaving him there with her, for days on end. His Uncle Adrian, Annie's brother, had stood in for the father he never knew. The other kids had teased him, saying his father was some old white drunk that his mother never called by name. This is a puzzle Omar has yet to put together. His Uncle Adrian had taught him to track deer, trap rabbits, and had helped to translate his visions. Leaning against the mnemonic tree, Omar wonders how his Nohkohmis will react when she knows he is home. He doesn't know that she has saved his sporadic letters from over the years, the ones written from jails and rooms above flashing lights; but she has saved them and reads them like books with pages missing. He expels the pine needle from between his teeth and begins walking resignedly down the hill.

While she prepares the berries for Ptakuwha, sour bread, steam from boiling deer meat permeates the house and makes sweat on the windows. Her purple hands work the dough, over and over. The same way her own mother and grandmother had done it. Her hands stop. For an instant she closes her eyes as if she could feel her face being brushed lightly with a feathered wing. Before submerging her hands in old dishwater, she mechanically glances out the window. She stands solemnly on the porch. Tears appear between the long grey braids that frame her face.

Omar munches on Ptakuwha and daqualaquay, closing his eyes with each bite. Nohkohmis lights the lamp. She begins a long recapitulation into a starry night once dominated by whippoorwills, owls, and coyotes. Omar's lips stumble over his first language. The good feel of the words thaw on his tongue, warming him like the closeness of Nohkohmis and the whitewashed log walls around them.

She lets him sleep this morning, until the humidity becomes too uncomfortable. Omar awakens, smearing the cool dampness over his body. He stretches his shoulders, rubs his face as if he were waking with a hangover. Realizing that he is at home, he lies still for a few moments longer, relieved. Omar knows it is hotter outside. He senses that his grandmother is not in the house. Putting on his pants, he walks to the screendoor, scans the summer light, sees her hoeing her rows of near mature corn. On her face, the sun reflects tiny beads of sweat. He can feel the sound of the hoe breaking the crust of rich bottomland earth and the clanging of steel when she strikes a rock. Remembering her words from the night, "Na quisah, my son, do you know why you have come home?" He didn't. And today is no different, not yet anyway. And one does not answer an elder haphazardly. Besides, Annie is from a generation that requires words straight from the heart. Their eyes cause lies to stumble.

Through the night hours, like pails of soil from a cave, she filled his absent seasons with past events: who had died, married, children born, feuds, illnesses, who was in jail, who got out, who moved away, moved home, powows, stomp dances, ball games, Green Corn Ceremonies, who was drinking, who had quit, who was off to college, who weren't raising their children right. All this before telling him about the lawyers from Tulsa, "The Greedy Ones are coming again."

They had told her that they were representatives of the Ozark Mining Company and that their mineralogists had tested the swampy bottoms for coal. The rich vein that they had found ran the whole length of the valley. Omar recalls her spitting motion as she related their promises of wealth to the Southwind People and all their descendants, if only they would sell their land for stripmining.

In his mind, Omar visualizes the nervous twitching of the attorneys as his grandmother patiently rebukes their attempts at cajoling her. She told them of the importance of the land, the children, and the ceremonies, ". . . . but their greed would not let them hear this truth." Mechanically, the attorneys repeated over and over the advantages that wealth could bring to a people. The attorneys, too, had tried to be patient. They raised their voices as if they were talking to a deaf person, one who could not hear that they were talking big bucks.

"The revenue from the coal will provide a lot of jobs for your people. Industry needs this coal. Take a little more time to think this over. We don't think you realize the magnitude of this situation. Other tribes have gladly sold leases to mine coal. They want to help out their country. They want businesses moving in on their reservations," said the one attorney whose fingers and neck were laden with turquoise jewelry.

"Yes," Annie had said, "Greed has affected lives among all the tribes. We heard Crows, Cheyennes, and Navajoes tell us stories about the coalmines. They say the big machines came and devoured the earth like angry monsters, spit out the remains and left orange water in their holes. They say their homes are gone, and their children are sick from the invisible enemy, their old people are turning to alcohol to bury the sorrow of their weaknesses, their ignorance in allowing this awful thing to happen. When our people make deals with you, there is only death. Your own history says it is so, yet you continue without regard for the balance of life. The sparkle of gold and silver is the light of your eyes. Go somewhere else and deceive some other people, like your fathers and mothers, but you will buy no land from the Southwind People." The red-faced attorneys had risen from their seats as if having been dealt a challenge rather than a refusal.

"Lady, we can see you need time to think this over. Here is some literature on coalmining. The land can be made to look as good as new and you can move back on it when the coal is dug out," said the turquoised one trying to control his thoughts.

"Now you speak of graveyards. Our home is alive now, and we will not sell our mother," Annie had spoken.

Truly frustrated, the attorneys stomped out the door promising Annie that they would be back with a more agreeable offer. She knew this was just the beginning. Omar shakes the conversation from his head.

Nohkohmis stands, the hoe supporting her folded hands, watching Omar leave the porch for the well. He has not forgotten how to sink a bucket and lift cold spring water to his lips. He sets the bucket down, splashes his face and chest. No words are necessary now. Nohkohmis knows. Omar knows. Behind the smokehouse, he takes a piss, watching the mid-day breeze play across the top of the sagegrass. It is the real world, the quiet world of beauty and daydreams. Omar thinks perhaps it is too quiet.

II

Days come and go, each one seeming to intensify with the heat. Omar passes time with his nohkohmis, with the intimacy of a first born grandson imitating the hands of his female blood. There is a noticeable absence of visitors that Omar attributes to the scalding heat, and does not verbally question this absence. But with his eyes, he questions her use of all these herbs that she is constantly collecting. Omar recalls many from his youth but has never realized the reasons for all the continual harvesting. Annie explains to him slowly and assuredly how to prepare the plants for medicine, that everything in this life is medicine if one knows how to use it properly.

"Even a small mistake may cause great harm to the user, and the one who prepares it. Many of the plants offer themselves at only one time during the seasons and if one is to use them, they must be taken at that time. One must never forget that, like all life, plants are male and female too, each giving according to its design. To take the plants or animals properly, you must know which side of you is required . . . . . ," Annie says, directing her statement deeply into Omar's presence, ". . . . This is the balance that Matche prevents others from knowing."

Omar becomes preoccupied with this balance. Even away from her, on White Bird Creek, swimming in the cold murky depth, "Each of us is male and female," she had said. Lying back in the shade of the bank, he stares into the river's hypnotic movement until he becomes an animate part of the beauty around him. A heated wind welters through the cottonwoods, shaking the willows as if someone were walking in them. It is the wind, and the heat and lack of rain that have lowered the creek.

It was like this, as a child, when his Uncle Adrian, other male relatives, and himself, would put seines at opposite ends of the creek, walk and swim them toward each other. Everyone would strip off their clothes, and with burlap sacks, dive into the water. Bodies would surface, yelling, "Hoyah, hoyah!" and laughing, everyone was always laughing, holding, grappling with bags of catfish, bass, and bluegill. Always at such gatherings, someone could be heard to say, "Giteen hili lewe! P'laytha hisip kihe!" P'laytha, the eagle, would always be circling, at first a mere speck in the humid sky, screaming, closer, watching, blessing. A fish from each bag was always left for P'laytha.

"Ah, yes, P'laytha," Omar remembers. It was about second or third grade, at the mission school. He was on these creek banks, in a confusion bordering on fear. He had been whipped again for quoting his methoshena, grandfather, "We don't need the Greedy Ones to tell us about our Creator. Great Eagle is our messenger between earth and sky. The Greedy Ones teach fear and hate. Our Creator is not such a one." The teachers had taken their turns whipping the young pagan into submissiveness.

With this recollection, Omar yet cringes. He can still feel the inward attack on his beliefs, his relatives, and shakes at the memory of the uncontrollable crying that overcame him when he looked to the sky to see many eagles circling. He remembers P'qway had been watching him from the opposite bluff. Omar's Methoshena Elmer had been fishing in the clearing above the willows, and had heard Omar's crying, "Miyon ne lahne, young man, what is the matter? Don't let P'qway hear you cry. It will make her sad." At that moment, P'qway had reared up on her haunches, her gentle black face appearing to smell the sky. Settling back on all four, she wandered the edge of the bluff, staring into the creek, until she was out of sight.

Omar gets up with his daydreams, wanders into the willows at the creek's edge. Stooping, he gouges out a ball of the blood red clay, and rolls it between his palms . . . . remembering his grandfather's stories of being at Carlisle Indian School in Pennsylvania where he had read the Bible. Elmer's teachers had smiled, well-satisfied that they were sending another heathen convert back to the wilds of Indian Territory. They became dismayed, however, to find that Elmer Blue Jacket, in reading the Bible, had only confirmed that the Creator of native people was the same one who had created the whiteman. The Creator had given to everyone, a place to live, and ceremonies that were in harmony with the homeland. That was why everyone was different. Aghast, the missionaries finally sent Elmer home, an unchangeable patron of Satan.

Through his remaining days, Omar's methoshena acted as a mediator between the Christian Indians and the traditional Round House people explaining that the Creator never intended for anyone to quarrel over religion, or to make war over interpretation. Omar recalls his grandfather's last speech at Green Corn, to peoples of both religions. "The elders speak of a time when we will live in peace and harmony with one another, again. They say our Creator will send the White Plumed Spirit back among us. In Europe's Bible, Jesus says, 'For as the lightning comes from the east and shines as far as the west, so will be the coming of the Son of man. Wherever the body is, there the eagles will be gathered together.'"

The ball of clay is nearly dry. "Omar!" Annie's voice interrupts his reminiscing. The clay ball rolls from Omar's long fingers into the creek, and dissolves. "Omar, the people are stomp dancing over in Bowleg's Hollow tonight. If you feel like it, we'll go. People have heard that you are home and have asked for you to come."

It is too sudden, the idea of going among the people. Other scenes flash through his head: hitchhiking into Newtown, to the night spots where white farmers elude Christian wives, where "Satin Sheets" is playing on the blue jukeboxes, guzzling beers over a pooltable . . . shit! Annie eyes him, back and forth, waiting for his reply.

"Damn!" he mumbles to himself. "How will we get there, Nohkohmis?"

"Your Uncle Adrian. He is coming in his truck, with his family. They all want to see you. They may come before dark, so come help me. There are things to do," she says, assuming an affirmation. The planning in Omar's eyes has not passed by her.

Western sky is fiery red when Omar hears the first whippoorwill near the house. A childhood excitement. Getting ready for a dance, almost like getting ready to go out to the bars. Omar feels slick. Just barely hanging over the collar of his white cowboy shirt, his sunburned black hair is parted in the middle and combed back behind his ears. He has two turquoise posts in his ears that were pierced by his grandmother when he was four. His sleeves are rolled to his elbows, exposing the tattoos on his forearms. On the right arm is an Indian with a western headdress, and the initials A.I.M. underneath; the left arm reveals the names, Roseanne, Naomi, Carol T., and a jumbling of initials, and scars that were desperate attempts at removing old initials, before adding new ones. His new looking blue jeans are boot cut and reach to the heel of beige colored boots with pointed brown tips like Navajos wear.

Annie, too, is busy. Moving about the house with premeditated opening and closing of drawers and cabinet doors. She holds first one shawl up to the remaining light, then another, with no pretense of hiding her excitement of attending the stomp dance with her beloved grandson . . . that his return might provide some kind of balance to their clan, and to this new threat from the stripmines, but for tonight, it is a dance. She continues with no other thought except for the wrapping of items that are without English names, into cloths of various colors. . . . "Omar, fold all those blankets and shawls that are in the front room closet, and put them into those garbage bags," she instructs him by pointing with her lips.

At that moment, Omar hears the motor rumbling across the field, iron breaking against stone. He sees the head-lights bouncing through the pines lining the rocky dirt road. Down into the dry wash and up, billows of red dust trailing into the yard, camouflaging headlights that have come to a dead stop. The back of the dark pickup is filled with kids, young men, and women, yelling and laughing at the wild horse ride.

Shadows dart about in the headlights. Omar walks into view. Shadows stand still. Silence. Omar, his hands in his back pockets, is nervously seeking familiarity. The driver's door opens and into view is Omar's Uncle Adrian. Silent words through eyes and smiles. Adrian Little Light, Kesauthwau, younger brother of Gonawah Hequawi, had assumed her husband's role of teacher for young Omar, after Elmer had died.

Omar searches his uncle's smooth brown face, the alert eyes that illuminate his tall, heavy, frame. His ungrayed black hair is short. Short, short, from boarding school days over sixty-one years ago. In the silence that occupies the space between Omar and Adrian, the power of Bear Clan reenters this circle, and it is like a dream that re-verses reality. Omar remembers the habits of two legs, four legs, and no legs, how their spirits return for food, for power, and how many others seek this knowledge to further control the lives of humans as well as animals, how Matche tries to weaken the clans so as to misuse their power. From all sides, come the odors of sage, sweetgrass, cedar, and Adrian's big hands and arms embracing Omar's stout body. In the firm embrace, Omar is finally connected with the old tobacco smell of his uncle, and the songs melt away the seasons of his thirty-two years.

Wanda, who is married to Adrian, gives the female embrace. She had provided shawls, food, and encouragement when Omar, as a child, had first danced. She is a mother who lines the road of harmony, whose face is always seen in the ring of firelight.

And the ancient presence that is inscribed into pottery and conch shell disks, that presided over councils atop archaic mounds lives inside Gonawah Hequawi. She stands, magenta Pendleton blanket, edged with black fringe, over her arm. On her feet are puckered style deerskin moccasins with a floral design in cut beads, barely perceptable beneath her long, blue broadcloth, transitional dress, edged with red, yellow, and green ribbon work. A handworked German-silver concho belt holds her waist. Her hair, unbraided, is wrapped behind her neck and hanging loosely past her waist. From each pierced ear hangs a German-silver waterbird. Suspended on a twisted string of sinew around her neck is a single bear's claw, usually worn only by males. There is neither modesty nor loftiness in her countenance, nor in Wanda's, or Adrian's, but Omar is inwardly trying to struggle loose.

He senses that there is something in tradition, in human memory that cannot be passed on without ceremony, cannot be recorded for history, but passes into the winds, into the soil and rivers until that time that someone must pick it up again, must use it to dignify survival, to give life to beauty. Omar cannot, does not allow himself to com-

plete his thoughts. He feels nauseous, like he must sit
down . . . . . .

Adrian comforts him, holding his arm under Omar's, "I
understand, Na quisah. It's been a long time . . . Maybe,
let's go fishing tomorrow, in old White Bird, huhhh! Let's
get everybody in the truck." Off to the side, yet embrac-
ing Omar, Adrian says to him, "You know, I bet we have
to cut switches to keep those Creek women off you
tonight. Aieeeee!"

Annie rides up front with Adrian, Wanda, and one small
grandson crying to ride in the back. Omar sits on blankets
in the truck bed with the younger relatives and their kids.
By tradition they are all brothers and sisters, nephews and
nieces, to Omar, but the years of absence brings only sur-
face conversation. Omar is glad to ride quietly through
the summer night, feeling the cool wind and looking up at
the stars. After leaving the dirt road, the truck turns onto
a county maintained gravel road along the foot of the
hills. The humid darkness rushes in on Omar reminding
him of the first time he hit Oklahoma City. "Damn! I
wish I had a good long swig of Jack Daniels," he says in
English to himself.

III

Woodsmoke permeates the air. The haunting swamp voice
of the lead singer, the steady rhythm of shakers, nostalgic
tremors possess Omar, momentarily, and again he realizes
that he dreams in someone else's sleep sometimes never
knowing which nightmare is real.

The grounds are lit with fires. German silver pendants
sparkle in the procession of dancers. Bright scarves hang
from necks, and suspend from clothing. Metal shakers,
attached to the legs of dancers, keep a constant beat with
singing and drumming.

Kids hurtle from the truck, and enjoy a momentary wild abandon scrambling between trucks and cars that have been battered by dirt roads and wired together beyond use by white people. Annie's family of Bear Clan people stand just long enough to groom themselves, and instruct the children before entering the grounds.

The song ends. Whispered conversations slow to a deafening silence. Children stop dead in their tracks to gape at the arriving delegation. The congregation observes with awe and admiration for one whose spiritual ties are unquestionable, and with curiousity for the mysterious grandson. An elder woman steps forward to shake hands with Gonawah Hequawi, then the others of her family. Other elders, mothers, fathers, and young people follow the elder lady in line, shaking hands with Bear Clan People, and welcoming Omar home. There are members of many tribes at this dance—Miamis, Creeks, Seminoles, Peorias, Delawares, Cherokees, Senecas, Shawnees— whose ancient homelands were east of the Mississippi River, until the resistance and removal days, all concentrated here in northeast Indian Territory. Now bound by blood ties and changing ceremonies.

In his mind, Omar realizes that his body and eyes move in "street fashion." He is glad to be here, but he is uneasy. He feels an odd sensation in his neck. The reverence shown for his grandmother, for him, is confusing. He wonders why he agreed to come. He shakes hands, tries to smile and return respect. As the greeters pass by, they begin resuming places. Adrian touches Omar's shoulder and motions with his lips toward a log bench.

Water drums begin warming up. Dancers file in two by two. Songs permeate veins of the forest until Omar gasps inside his former world. Drums resound inside his head, his chest, from times surviving in warrior hearts. At eighteen he had simply shrugged when his friends had spoken

of joining the army . . . to become warriors. His grand-
father, Elmer, had said that he thought young people in
these days had begun to believe what the whites had writ-
ten in their history books about Indians. All that bullshit.
Why should a real warrior offer his life to defend the
enemy, Matche, who continued to drain the very life from
his own people, and the land? Omar is a warrior. Deep in
his blood, he has always known it, but the frustration of
not knowing what all this blood means. . . .

"What does it mean to be a warrior?" he had asked his
grandfather.

"To be honorable," his grandfather had said, "and to
pray for honor among all our relatives."

What was honor? Omar had left home for reasons not
even known to himself. The ambiguous term, job reloca-
tion, had gotten lost in the gloomy shadows of bars, and
in the people who lived in those bars. Many times while
drunk, Omar had tried to figure it out. He told himself
that this was why he stayed drunk so often. Then he
would use it as an excuse for sobering up, then use it for
getting drunk again.

Omar recalls that in desperate moments of his street
world, drunk and screaming hopelessly for a touch of rec-
ognition, he would fall into his stinking sweat, wake up in
dark rooms bare of surroundings. In the corner of dark-
ness, he would hear grunting and snorting, a bear licking
its paws as if they were greasy. In pounding silence, he
would attempt to focus on the bear's figure, but he can
never recall being awake when the dank gamboling animal
approached him.

Adrian's hand rests reassuringly on Omar's. "Son, you're
home. Stay here with us. Your grandmother needs you at
home. She is getting on in her days, worries about those
lawyers."

Omar quickly changes the subject with, "Uncle, who was my father? Why has no one ever spoke of him to me? I'm grown man. What kind of secret can change my life at this time?"

"Because I only know what others tell me regarding those days, you must seek this information from your nohkoh-mis . . . the story is too unclear for me to attempt to clear your mind on who your father was," Adrian concluded. Omar stares at his uncle with a smiling resignation and gets up to walk around the dance grounds.

Groups of young girls who had timedly shaken hands with Omar, are now following him as he walks. He turns abruptly, grunting out, "Yahhhh-eh!" The girls scream. . . . laughing. .

And boldly whisper to each other and yell loudly, "Aieeeee . . ." They do this over and over. Someday one of these girls will snag him. They think.

Omar shakes hands with old school chums, cousins, their children and appears to be talking intimately with some of the guys, and those young girls still flashing black shining eyes back and forth. Annie, visiting with a group of shawled older women on the other side of the dance, watches everything.

Leaving her friends with an indication of return, Annie catches up to Omar, and instructs him to aid his uncle in bringing up the plastic bags from the truck.

Wanda, Adrian, Omar, and cousins bring the bags of blankets, shawls, food, and lay them near the big fire. Wanda and Annie spread thin cotton blankets on the ground. All the blankets and shawls are stacked neatly on top with several bags of food, including chunks of fresh beef from Adrian's herd, laid out on the plastic.

All singing has stopped. The headman of the dance grounds calls for all family members of Gonawah Hequawi and Kesauthwau to come forward and assist their relatives in the give away. Annie instructs the standing positions of everyone. Her brother Kesauthwau and his family on her left. Omar stands on her right. Annie begins, "Na quisah, Omar, has come home to be with his people. Since this is so, it is the way of our clan that we show our happiness in this fashion. Kesauthwau will call out the names to come up and receive a gift from our family. When we have called all the names, those visitors and ones who did not hear their names will please come and accept the remaining gifts."

Each recipient passes, shaking hands first with Omar, then each member on down to the youngest child. After all the gifts are taken, the lead singer begins a song accompanied by other singers and the drummers and dancers. Omar and his family must lead. This is familiar to Omar, who has forgotten all about wanting a drink, and is feeling the drum in his feet. Males, side by side, followed by females. . . . in the center of night . . . seeming tireless . . . like the singers whose voices are more explicit as daylight, pale and irrefutable, appears above hills to the east, edging into the starry sky.

The morning star hears the laughing, last minute visiting . . . shines into the open mouths of children whose eyes are sealed. . . . blankets shake into morning air. . . . teasing . . . laughter. Hosts of the stomp dance grounds smother the fires. Annie quietly packs a sleeping child into the truck and gets in beside him. First light of sun breaks through the dust and onto the stomp grounds. Silence. The embers are dead, but the earth is resonating long after everyone is gone. It is another humid day.

IV

In the house, Annie and Wanda are busy frying bread, potatoes, and some of the fresh beef that Adrian had brought. Two of Wanda's daughters-in-law are washing dishes and pans as they are dirtied. While the other males and young children are sleeping, Adrian and Omar chop kindling for the cookstove. The day is becoming unusually hot and steamy. Omar feels his uncle's unspoken concern for the days ahead. Cicadas, or jarflies as children call them, are especially loud . . . in the cottonwood trees. Since coming home, Omar's body has tanned into a coffee brown, perspiration trickles down crevices of his firm muscles. Glaring below the wet brow of his uncle, Omar says, "I think this is enough wood to keep 'em cooking all week. I'll be back later, Uncle." With this, Omar lodges his axe into an oak log, and heads across the field to White Bird Creek. His steady gait over the hill is marked by Annie's watching form standing in the window until he is out of sight.

Omar spends the rest of the day sleeping in the shade of a hickory grove above the falls. Into late evening, the constant rushing water and old songs are in his dreams. He distinguishes a vague image of his grandfather. It was near this spot, before he could walk upright, that his grandfather had shaved baby Omar's head, speaking native words to him through song, then submerging him many times into the creek.

A cool breeze comes sweeping off the water, low rumbling rolls over the hills to the east. A molten gray spreads across the sky. Physically awakened by Semyalwa's voice, urgently loud, Omar crawls from his sleep to the water's edge.

As he splashes his face, Omar notices that the water has lost its clearness and is floating pieces of debris. To the east, he sees the streaks of summer lightning breaking holes in massive dark clouds. Semyalwa's hooting stirs his memory. He is beginning to react to the sounds and signs of this earth as if he has never left it. "What the fuck! What in hell is wrong with me anyway?" Something is not right and he senses the alarm inside himself is real. Like a buck with its white tail high, Omar leaps across the rocky terrain up through the last patch of sunlight on the hill.

From the cedared hill above the house, Omar sees a strange truck parked in Annie's yard. Two whitemen are idling near the rear of the truckbed. A large framed man is sitting on the steps, with Annie upright behind him, hands on her hips. Each gestures wildly as they speak. Suddenly the big man, his face shaded by a baseball cap, stands up to face Annie. Both are hand talking frantically. There is a momentary hesitation between them. The old Indian stare off. The big man rubs his hand across his face, lifts Annie by her shoulders, and heaves her big-boned body off the porch and into the yard where she sprawls, motionless. Blood spurts through Omar's veins, spontaneous aim guides his footsteps, his race down the hillside, his voice that is ranting like an MGM Indian, the valley becomes liquid before his eyes.

"Windell, someone's coming down the hill," shouts one of the idling whitemen. The two idlers leap into the truck, spinning red soil into the air, and yelling for Windell to hurry up.

Windell hesitates over Annie's unconscious body as if there is something else he needs to do. He looks to the hillside at Omar's approaching form, not knowing for certain. He hears the thunder and breaks for the truck. The truck skids into the arroyo, and up onto the dirt road. Windell slams the door . . . The curly black hair, fluffed out from under the baseball cap on Windell's big head, is barely visible to Omar. And to Windell, Omar is a fading form in the thick dust.

Omar races on into the yard where Annie is sitting up gasping for air. "Nohkohmis, Nohkohmis. . . . ," Omar pleads.

"Let me catch my breath, Naquisah. . . .Uhnh . . ahhnh, . . . Help me up here," Annie says as Omar helps settle her on the porch.

"You're hurt, I'll run for Uncle Adrian."

"No, no," Annie interjects, "I'm not hurt; just out of breath. You sit down here beside me and be quiet. . . ," Annie commands.

"Well, what the hell is going on here?" Omar says impatiently. "Who comes here to make a fight with an old woman?"

Annie puts her head down as if she is not going to reply. Then gets up with a stagger, balancing herself on a porch post, and asks Omar, "Do you remember Windell Osborne from when you were in high school at Newtown?"

"I remember the name."

"Ohhh, his mother was Renee White Hoof, a tribal member who years ago took up with one of those railroad workers from Kansas. She had Windell, and when he was about three or four, he watched his dad beat his mother until she died. You were just a young child then. Windell's father claimed she had been sneaking out on him and sleeping around with Indians which was a lie cause all she did was try to keep peace with her relatives who knew that he was no damn good. An he was no damn good," Annie speaks with a bitter tremor in her voice. "He left Windell in Newtown with that no good drinking white trash that let Windell grow up like a wild dog and ashamed, hating the Indian part of himself. Windell's father was always running around with Indian girls who hang in those bars up there. Some say he took off to Montana with some Crow girl during Anadarko Fair. He's probably dead by now, but Windell is just like him."

"Yeah, I remember him now," Omar relates. "He always ran with whites and I remember him calling Indian girls, 'whores.' He never did speak to me, but would pass in the hallways as if he didn't see me. There were always some guys like that. But there was this one time when no one was around. He was standing around on the back stairs smoking a cigarette, he turned around, our eyes met as if we recognized each other for the first time. I felt funny, you know, sort of helpless or something. He just threw his smoke away and went on. How come he attacked you, Nohkohmis?"

"The coal lawyers sent him and those two drunks out here to talk to me about selling our land to the stripminers. He told me how he never had nothing all his life, and how rich we would be if we would deal with the lawyers. When he finished talking, I spoke to his heart, told him to come back here among his mother's people, go into the sweat-lodge, and pray for his spirit to return. We talked about his past, and the confusion that living like whites brings to a human being. Then he jumped up with that deadly look in his eyes and said that 'no damned Indian witch was going to keep him from getting what was owed to him.' When he was holding me by my shoulders, I spit bitter root into his face. Then he hurled me to the ground, knocked the breath out of me."

"That sonofabitch," Omar speaks intently, turns around and runs into the house. He gathers from his bag what few bucks he has and flies out the door with Annie on his heels.

"Son, what are you doing? Na quisah, I am not hurt. What do you. . . . . ."

"Nohkohmis, that man will not let this be the last of his visits. He will not treat my grandmother or any of my people in this manner. I'm not going to let him get away with this."

"Oh, son, Windell and those men will kill you. They are not warriors. They are like wild dogs . . . don't go up there . ." Annie's pleading, the wisdom of time, trails through deaf ears. She sees into Omar's world, and that he is going to do what he has decided. A sense of the past runs before her eyes as she watches one side of his spirit prepare itself. There is no separating the two storms that have now entered the valley.

V

Inside the car, the driver is a shadowy figure to whose conversation Omar replies automatically. Driving is slow as the headlights cannot penetrate the blowing sheets of rain pelting the windshield, jetting the blacktop, deluging the years of turmoil that drives Omar's spirit. He recalls many dark nights just like this one. Hitching to some-where, anywhere, creating his own purpose as he went. Many times he would do the driving for whoever picked him up. They would sleep and he would drive for hours and hours, maybe days, through sundown and sunup, sometimes popping those little white crosses. If he were lucky, he would find some wild soul like himself who would have plenty of money, booze, and speed. He sure liked tearing through the nights like that. But, on this cruise, there is a difference. Sitting back, staring at his reflection in the passenger's window, he is beginning to suspect what that difference is.

Newtown, population 5,280, western gateway to the Ozarks, was once a boomtown during the oil discovery days. But the oil has played out except for a few auto-matic wells rusting in barren fields, perpetually pumping and draining the last bit of life from the earth. They remind Omar of those little bird thermometers in roadside cafes, forever bending over, touching the water and bouncing up. The last days of the oil had been crazy days for everyone, including the Indians. Some of whom had sold leases on their allotments. Omar remembers when Indians first drove automobiles in this region. Cars, bright and shiny one day, were smashed up the next. Sometimes, in town, people would forget where they parked. So what? Just go buy another one. Out of gas? Hook up a team of horses to the car, take the family shopping. White folks shook their heads, but kept on grinning as long as the cash was coming in. The same grinning white folks whose lives revolved around churches, whorehouses, and bars. In Newtown, they were born together creating the largest realm of social activities that now remain.

Farmers, ranchers, land speculators, and a few tourists keep the Newtown food stores, the Texaco gas station, and the courthouse, alive. Presently, a new excitement runs through the feeble minds of its citizens. Coal is going to restore Newtown to its past days of glory. Omar's eyes latch onto the yellow and green neon sign with the rock-holed, neon, bubbling martini glass, and blue neon olive. Cocktails. Country Palace. Omar recalls a guy at the stomp dance telling him about this joint, and the fights in the parking lots.

Inside, the country-western band's lead singer drones out, "Burning memories, teardrops fall when I have burning memories." It is the same band that Omar has seen in a hundred places like this one. They wear the same sequined outfits, move their lips like Porter Wagoner with the same "good ole boy" smiles. Sawdust floors, cowboy hats, boots, and rodeo buckles. Omar walks idly through, nodding to Indians lining the bar. Momentarily, he searches the tightly woven faces at the round wooden tables where brown bottles stand like stalagmites in a cave. No familiar face. Omar heads for the toilet. Inches of water and piss cover the cement floor. A roll of toilet paper is clogging the stool, yet people continue to piss in it.

Cowboys coming in to drain beer from overstuffed guts drunkenly bump Omar from the long trough where he is pissing. He recognizes the smell of this place in a thousand scenes. He has felt his own blood spilling in these toilets. For some reason now, he feels a strange sense of disgust, fed up with being goaded into fights over someone bumping into him, fed up with eye level graffitti that reads, "Niggers are living proof that Indians fucked buffaloes". The minds of colonial America are inscribed on bathroom walls. In past drunken stupors he had even written there himself. With a bemused smile, he shakes the moisture from his dick, purging past offenses that carry no meaning on a warrior's road. He wonders about the encounter, seeing Windell Osborne after all these years.

Omar walks boldly to the bar where eyes try to place his origin and wonder who he's looking for. In his mind, Omar knows he wants a shot, or even a can of beer. Here, where he can smell alcohol, revenge does not seem as important as it did this afternoon, even though his heart tells him that he must be sober when he faces Windell. Somehow he knows that he is facing a part of himself, himself as a human being, as a Bear Clan descendant. As a grandson of Gonawah Hequawi. He thinks he will order a coke. And visit with all the "skins" here at the bar and when they say, "Gosh, guy, what you drinking?", he'll just tell them that he's going to AA or something. Lot of guys do that, but why can't he say that alcohol is not a tradition, even though we have let the alcohol convince us otherwise. What is that shame in refusing a drink?

"Yoko heights, my friend. Where you from?" The ques-

84

tion shakes Omar from his dilemma. Without waiting for an answer, Arlen extends his hand, volunteering, "I'm Arlen Koomsity, Kiowa-Comanche, from Lawton. Now you look lost, Jack. What's eating you?" Arlen portrays a similar configuration of facial scars and features as does Omar, scars from dubious wars and a bulb that once was a well formed nose. He seems taller, wearing his hair in two lengths of immaculate braids reaching just below his waist.

Omar is caught in the first sensation of polarity since coming home, and cannot drop his gaze from Arlen's trenchant black eyes. It is a welcome feeling. He returns Arlen's wide smile. "Sorry Bro, I guess I'm still somewhere else," Omar says, holding the handshake for an instant longer. "My name's Omar Little Light, from over on White Bird Creek."

"Might know, aieeee. . . ," Arlen jokes in a way that only tribal people do, "another one of them eeeastttern tribes, aiieeee."

"Fuck you too, Jack," Omar pretends to be seriously angry, "At least I don't run around with scabby asshole, or talk Indi'n with a Spanish accent."

"Ooooohhhh, damn guy! What kind of Indian can't take a joke? What's going on with you anyway?"

"Oh, shit, guy, that's too long a story for now. What brings you over here among us eeeastttern tribes, anyway?" Omar asks in a more serious tone.

"Oooh, hell! Got kicked out by my Creek woman over by Henrietta about a week ago. Shit, I wasn't ready to go back to Lawton. Know me too good over there . . . aieeeee. Thought I'd stay here and try to snag around. It's hell, too, trying to find a job. These white folks here are strange, Jack. Supposed to go Friday and help this one guy load some stock. Damn, here, have a beer."

Omar takes the beer, knowing that it is contrary to his purpose, his warrior spirit . . . but. . . . . . But he has just met a friend. They will get drunk together, be just like old times with other barroom friends. Hell, it's raining outside, probably won't see Windell anyway. Omar sips the beer. Good and warm to his throat, to his belly, takes the rest in one long swallow.

"Damn, brother, there's more," Arlen says. Arlen knows that there is something going on in Omar's world, but in this world one waits for the right time to speak. Arlen turns, orders two more Coors. "Colorado Kool-aid. Got used to this shit drinking with those Indians in Albuquerque, 49ing up on the cliffs. Damn rugged bunch out there."

Omar stands, sipping this time, watching the door, relaxing next to Arlen, talking powows and people with whom they have crossed paths. Many beers later, he and Arlen decide on a change of pace. Across the street and down to the Tropical Zone.

It's still pouring rain. Unconcerned about getting drenched, Omar looks down at his feet. His boots, ankle-deep reservoirs; he knows he is getting drunk again. Feels like that time in Portland on Skid Row. He was looking at his bare feet then. Someone had stolen his boots during the hour before daylight. He had turned his head sideways and laughed at himself. Walking barefoot through the black veins of Portland's gutters.

"Damn you, you motherfuckers," Arlen curses a truck that splashes him in a deliberate swerve through the flooded streets. The incident is barely audible to Omar. The truck angle parks in front of the Tropical Zone where Omar and Arlen are headed. Truck doors fly open. Three men stumble out oblivious to the torrential runoff that fills their boots.

"Windell, you sonofabitch, you made me spill this beer all over my crotch," one of the trio rages.

Windell! The name tears through Omar's stupor. He looks up. Focuses. Their eyes meet. Windell senses the familiar eyes. . but he does not know. The rain that has cooled the summer swelter, and coming face to face with Windell causes the fog to lift from behind Omar's eyes.

"Hehhhhenh, you crazy bastard, everybody knows you're always pissing on yourself anyway. Who cares if it's piss or beer?" Windell says, slamming shut the truck door dismissing the drunk standing out in the street. Windell gaits toward the bar, his two companions following. Ted, his big nose protruding from beneath his Schlitz cap, walking bowlegged, is still laughing at Floyd and pointing to the black dampness on his green pants.

It is all that Omar can do to restrain Arlen from blasting right into the three assholes who have drenched him. Omar grabs Arlen by the shoulders and says, "Neegi, friend, this is not the time. . I was going to tell you later, when we sobered up. This is why I am here in town. Those three dudes have got more friends inside that bar. I want the big one myself, the one who threw the water up on you. Trust me. I'm not lookin' to get us both killed."

"The right way is just to do it, bro. I ain't used to having white people treat me like I was a damn alley cat . . . no way, Jack. . . ."

"Arlen, there's just more to this than you know. Trust me guy. I'm not a coward," Omar is saying the words aloud, and silently. He is trying to remove his mission from becoming a barroom brawl, he tells himself trying to lift his spirit into a proper motion, but this goddamn alcohol. All he wants to do tonight is drink and be with Arlen. Proper revenge will have its time.

"Come on, Arlen, let's go shoot some pool. See if you Kiowas are any good . . . aieee." Arlen smiles into Omar's challenging grin. Arlen likes Omar and is beginning to sense that inside Omar is a native respect that is passed on only by those who have remained loyal to their elders. Whether they are drinkers or strict traditional people, it is the respect that matters, that holds native people apart from the foreigners in this land.

Omar feels a strange contentment, even though the memory of the afternoon burns deeply inside him. A hundred years ago he imagines Arlen leading young men out to steal horses from the Mexicans and landgrabbers, herding them wildly across the plains. Omar recalls childhood stories of the people being moved at bayonet point from the Ohio Valley, the ferocity of the English soldiers, trained murderers, killing and burning, and the names are yet alive of the brave men and women who tried vainly to defend their families and the land. Omar has an ally, and shoulder to shoulder they carry their thoughts across the street.

The Tropical Zone is a typical dive: three rugged looking pool tables, iron folding chairs and card tables, one long L-shaped bar, and nothing breakable but the bottles from which hardcore patrons drink. Windell, Ted, and Floyd are at the back pool table, laughing and cutting up with two Indian girls. A cold sensation passes through Omar, seeing those girls hanging with Windell's crowd, but he's seen it before. He, himself, knows that alcohol chooses companions that will perpetuate its addictive powers. The bar reeks of stale alcohol that has hit the floor in hundreds of brawls. Windell looks up again to stare questioningly at Omar who pretends not to notice. Instead he walks over and puts a quarter on the table next to Windell's.

"Watsa' matter with you two chiefs? 'Fraid to put yer quarter up over here against us white boys?" Ted asks in a provokingly southern drawl.

Omar glances over to Arlen who nods approvingly. "Sure," Omar says, "no women or kids here . . . just warriors." Ted and Floyd wink at each other, then finish out their game.

"Rack 'em boys!" Floyd commands. Arlen and Omar size up the pool sticks that Arlen declares are shaped like a dog's hind leg. As Omar racks up the balls, he watches Windell who has positioned himself at the bar, stooping over a bottle of Old Yellowstone and mumbling to some other predators who are keeping a corner eye on the game about to begin.

Floyd and Omar flip for the break. Omar wins on tails. Before Omar breaks, Floyd asks, "Do y'all wanna put some money on this game? Say Five?"

Arlen again nods a consent to Omar, and asks, "Sure y'all can afford it?" They each show their money. Omar breaks and the eight ball sinks deadly into the right corner pocket.

Standing aside, Omar reaches for the five from gaping Ted and winks at Arlen who carries that same wide smile. "Rack 'em, boys," Omar triumphantly orders.

They continue playing, almost to closing time. Omar's years around a pool table is more than Ted and Floyd can stand, and Arlen's past life in the City and hustling coins at Anadarko, visibly angers Floyd. He positions the butt of his pool stick, ready to swing. Ted quickly grasps Floyd in a bear hug, whispering loudly in Floyd's ear, "Not now . . not now . . . catch 'em some other time," suggestively staring into Floyd's face.

"Catch us now, motherfuckers . . ." Arlen threatens as he moves toward Floyd, but is interrupted by Omar.

"We got their money, Jack. Let 'em go. If the bartender calls the cops, it'll be us they throw in jail . . ." Omar says pleadingly to Arlen, who also knows this is a statement of fact. It just always seems that whatever a native person holds to be honorable and just, the whiteman can look into his books and find where the native is breaking the law. This realization comes to Arlen in his external world for the first time. He backs off.

Ted and Floyd buy themselves an illegal six pack and leave, looking back only long enough to assure themselves that Arlen is not on their asses.

"Damn it. . . . where's Windell . . . fuck! . . I wasn't watching . . he's gone!" Omar rushes to the door, surveying both ends of the street. It has stopped raining but lightning is still streaking like snakes' tongues above the hills southeast of town. Windell's truck is gone. Omar stands, weaving back and forth.

"Hey, bro, now what the fuck's wrong with you? He ain't going nowhere. A hog never wanders far from its trough. That guy looks like he's part Ind'n . . . is he?"

"His mom was an Indian."

"Come on back in here, bro, and let's drink another one before they throw us out," Arlen says, realizing that Omar is too wasted to wander around looking for revenge on somebody.

Back inside, they huddle smoking cigarettes and sipping beer until the bartender gives the absolute and final last call. Omar has drunkenly related the visits of the strip-mine lawyers and Windell's part in all this and how it has been coming back to his relatives, living like they live, and his grandmother, his uncle and the beatings he got at the mission school, jails, how he had never had a woman who really felt good to him.

As they were standing to leave, Arlen says, "Shit, Omar, don't take all this crap by yourself. I'm your bro, guy. We'll find that sonofabitch tomorrow . . . when we've sobered our asses up. You know somebody we can stay with here . . . or is there a party, aieee? Shit, let's get out of here anyway," Arlen says, with his arm around Omar's back guiding him toward the door.

Omar, barely able to hold his eyes open, is thinking that he never wants his nohkohmis to see him like this . . . ever. The words she would have to say, he never wanted to hear. Maybe he would start dancing again after he had settled this business with Windell. He was about to ask Arlen if he were a dancer, but then, Arlen, being a Kiowa, would tell him that he was the best fancy dancer that ever hit the plains. They all say that. Maybe he and Arlen could hit the summer powow circuit together, head up into the Dakotas, show those Siouxs a thing or two. Damn drunk thinking.

They head down the back stairs, bumping into each other as they stumble. Omar lifts his bloodshot eyes just far enough to make out the piss and beer stains on Floyd's green pants. . . . .

VI

Storm clouds hang, imperceptibly blue, over Newtown. It has started drizzling rain again. A long line of dark grey clouds lie banked over the hills to the southeast. Omar senses the wet earth beneath him, feeling the stiffness in his face, the thundering in his belly. He can smell the blood tightening in his nostrils. "What alley is this," he thinks as he tries picking the congealing blockage from his nose so that he can breathe. Around ruptured veins of his eyes, the narrow slits gradually unseal the mucus. Lips wince as he touches the bulging blackness around them and his eyes. Arlen! Where is Arlen?

"Arlen!" Omar barely coughs aloud the name. "Arlen, where are you?" From the soggy heap of cardboard boxes, Omar sees the back of Arlen's form lying in the cerulean haze. "Arlen! Brother . . . get up!" Omar lifts Arlen's blue, swollen hand, gently rubbing its taunt flesh. "Brother," Omar is almost whispering. Arlen's neck is bloated, purple, and limp. The air is cool. Its wetness has already absorbed the warm brown from Arlen's face. "No . . oh, no, Gitghe Manido. . . . . no . . . no . . . no. . . ." Omar backs upright. Begins fighting unseen enemies. Stumbling over cans and bottles scattered about the alley, he cries out with a furor that had fled him when he first returned to the depths of White Bird Creek. His brain aches with a thousand screams in the world of blue shadows. A strong gust blows up the alley . . . Coyotes laughing. . . . "Windell!"

Omar feels the earth tremble beneath as he kneels by Arlen's body: "I never meant to bring you to this, brother. It was brief, yoko heights . . . I will see you someday again," Omar says, scooping up a chunk of the coral mud. . . . and with his finger, smears a streak across Arlen's face . . . and his own.

Omar plods into the blue dawn. "Nohkohmis . . . where are you, Gonawah Hequawi?" He becomes numb inside. The physical pain blots into the past. Omar staggers toward the edge of town.

Omar is standing, thumb out. No rides in his condition. He continues walking. Past the Twilight Motel. He stops . . . as if there were a diamondback at his feet. Windell's truck is parked in front of cabin 7. He could never forget that truck, the one that had drenched Arlen, the one that had left his grandmother laid out in her front yard, the truck that was destined for the whiteman's Hell.

Looking left, then right, Omar surveys the area as if he already has a plan. He feigns to be drunk, inconspicuously paces his way near the cabin . . . noticing that the old wooden planks are long in need of painting. He listens. Hears nothing. The blinds are closed. He assumes they are sleeping off their victorious drunk. Casually, Omar tries the door. It is open. In the dark, he distinguishes the form of a hairy butted white man . . . motionless on a bed. In the other bed, is the naked shadow of a man humping a girl, probably one of the girls from the bar last night.

"Goddamnit, man, shut that fuckin' door!" It is Windell's voice, thinking that big nosed Ted is back with more beer.

Omar quietly shuts the door, walks around to the truck, keeping an eye for Ted. Silently, he opens the truck, gets in, puts it in neutral, gets out, begins pushing it out of the parking lot. After pushing the truck from hearing distance of the cabin, he gets back in, tears out two wires from beneath the dash and begins sparking them together until the truck is started. He begins a song under his breath, humming at first, then gradually raising the crescendo until it sounds as if two high pitched voices are singing in unison.

The singing stops abruptly. Omar sits quietly for a moment revving up the engine, watching. At the critical moment, big nosed Ted comes from the side of the motel office, carrying a sack of beer: "Hey, hey, you sonofabitch. What are you doing? Hey, you'd . . ." Ted's approach is too late.

The truck peals out spitting blasts of mud and creosote gravel. The cabin comes before Omar's eyes like his dreams of driving over the edges of cliffs. In his ears, he can hear the slow cracking of glass and planks, splinters of cabin kindling float through motionless air, voices yelling under the soft crunch of flesh and bones as the truck comes to an unceremonious halt under piles of debris and upended mattresses.

Ted lifts his cap, his eyes like silver dollars glaring over his giant red nose, in awe as the plaster and sawdust settle in the humid air. The engine revs up again, begins backing out of the wreckage onto the blacktop parking lot. Through grey clouds reflecting in the spiderweb of the windshield, Ted recognizes Omar's battered face. "Goddamn. . . ," is all he can say as the truck begins speeding toward him. Cans clink, rolling over the asphalt, and explode under the wheels of Windell's truck. Ted is running for his life, gasping for the heavy oxygen, and somersaults himself into the sewage ditch beyond a telephone pole.

Omar slides the truck sideways without visibly stopping. Gears grind . . . and the sirens . , . red lights flashing coming from the north, barreling down on the arena. Omar knows he must be free to take his revenge. He continues his direction toward the south, then cuts east through town to throw the cops off his trail should they decide to pursue him.

By the time that Ted reaches the devastation, Windell is surfacing from the cavity, naked and bleeding, tripping and falling toward Ted. "What in hell . . . was . . . that . . ?" Windell utters, groaning out to Ted. Ted grabs Windell before he falls again.

"Goddamn . . . Windell . . . you best lie down here until the ambulance comes . . . you might be bleeding or broken up inside. That cut across you face looks bad . . . let me see if I can find something to stop the bleeding." Ted picks up a sheet and applies it to Windell's face.

"Here comes the cops, Ted . . . see if you can find my pants in that mess . . . see if Floyd is still alive."

"Windell, the guy in your truck is one of those guys we

beat up in the alley last night . . . that was shooting pool with me and Floyd in the bar."

"Who the hell is that guy?" Windell searches silently in his mind. For an instant, he looks into those eyes again on the steps of Newtown High School. He recalls the rumor from the white people who had reared him of his dad runnng off with another Indian woman who was from White Bird Creek. His brain explodes almost audibly, "I'll be damned. So that's who that is . . damn, I should have known . . . coming down the hill yesterday. Old Annie's grandson!"

The four state police officers stand gawking at the mess, puzzling at Windell's naked body. The tall, potbellied lieutenant, in his khaki dress and wide-brimmed hat, appears somewhat concerned. "Are there other people in thaerr?" he asks.

Ted is searching the rubble for Floyd. "Yeah, our buddy and his girlfriend are in here somewhere." The other three officers begin lifting away pieces of plank, and blankets. Floyd's shining bald head is exposed . . . still passed out, but alive.

One of the officers finds a pair of pants and tosses them to Windell. By this time, other motel patrons are standing and watching from their doors . . . too uneasy to approach the demolition. The lieutenant states, "There is an ambulance on its way. You guys sit down here and keep yourselves covered until they arrive."

"Lieutenant! Lieutenant! Come here and look at this!" one of the officers excitedly commands. Floyd is sitting upright and beginning to come around. The officer is holding up a mattress just a few feet from Floyd . . . the girl is lying half into the rut of the floor, entrails and blood oozing from her mouth . . . her anus . . her vagina. Her eyes are still open . . . staring motionless into the faces around her.

"Holy shit," the lieutenant conveys his first vocal emotion. He takes off his hat and is rubbing the yellow burr of his head. "What the hell is going on around here today? We just picked up another dead Ind'n back of the Tropical Zone about an hour ago. Y'all wouldn't know anything about that, would you?" the lieutenant directs at the trio. "What's going on here anyway? Who was driving that truck that blazed off from here awhile ago?"

Windell discreetly elbows Ted, and says, "His name is Omar Little Light, Old Annie's grandson from out on White Bird Creek. He was on a tear through town here last night. Last I heard, he was in prison somewhere. Probably got out not too long ago."

"What's his connection with you?" the lieutenant asks, staring intently through his sunglasses.

"Him and some Indian guy, probably the guy you found behind the bar this morning, were arguing over whose girl this was . . . this here girl that's layin' here dead. . . . Me and my buddies here tol' him to take it outside . . . I'd say that was what happened to that dead Ind'n. Omar probably killed him. Anyway we tell this girl to come with us, and she'd be safe from both of 'em. Near as I can figger, he was headin' home and saw our truck parked here at the motel, looked in at us cause the door was unlocked, and saw her with us. He's a damn alky anyway. Got it in his head to drive my truck through the front of the cabin, then took off probably headin' for the city where he's got friends that will hide him. There's no telling what he's liable to do once he gets where he can start drinkin' again . . . or smoking that marijuana." Windell's story seems together. His companions nod in agreement as he speaks.

Removing his sunglasses temporarily, the lieutenant asks, "Uh huh . . . Describe your truck to me, Windell."

"It's a 1964, GMC, half-ton, dark brown, with some of the front end smashed up very likely."

While the lieutenant is on his car radio, the ambulance arrives. As the girl's body is being loaded, the officer returns to where Windell is standing. "Well, we got an APB out on your truck. I think you guys better ride with the ambulance and get those cuts taken care of. Your partner there might be injured worse than he looks."

"Naw, he's alright. Ain'tcha Floyd?" Floyd nods affirmatively. "What we need is some rest. Floyd's old lady will come pick us up . . and patch this cut for me. I take it, you're going after that guy and get my truck back for me?" Windell asks, the ears behind his green, fox-like eyes, lying back.

"Yeah, we're going to follow up on the Tulsa road to make certain he hasn't turned off somewhere, and if there's no sign, we'll go out by his grandma's place later. I don't believe he would head there right away, probably after dark. You guys get home and lie in some hot water, and we'll come by to see how you're getting along later this evening."

VII

Omar drives east through town to confuse the cops. Maybe they will think he is hiding in town, or will cut north to Tulsa, or west to the City, but he heads south on the Starr blacktop. He turns off on the dirt road that leads to Golden Hole, a commonly known fishing area of White Bird Creek.

He parks the truck on the hill overlooking the creek where it is wide and quiet except for the lapping sound rising on the banks from the runoff. He is alone. Rain begins falling, lightly . . again . . . but like it does in early autumn. Veins of white plaster streak the shattered windshield of Windell's truck. Omar gets out, walks solemnly down the hill on the well worn path. He can hear the roaring of the falls about one half mile upstream. Omar continues until he comes in full view of the falls. He discovers the shallow overhang, covered with brush, that had been another of his secret places many years ago.

All this chaos is more traumatic than anything he can remember on the streets. Away from home, he had learned to look over the horror of living in a world created by greed. And staying drunk had helped, but here, it is different. Or is it? His people are in this region because of greed, and here they yet remain devoted to values given to them by the Creator.

It is this very spot where Omar had fallen asleep when he was twelve years of age. He'd thought he was asleep, but his drowsy head had lifted and was watching a form taking human shape in the mist of the falls. An old time appearing warrior had come wading from the water, his center hair unshaven, his face with the brillance of youth, strength, and courage. The aroma of the musky hollows had surrounded his sinewy body. Around the warrior's neck hung a long used bear claw necklace that Omar seemed to think familiar, but could not remember. The man stood over Omar's body and pursed his lips exultingly. He wore only a breechcloth. Omar knew the face, the eyes, but he had no words of cognition; he only knew that he was not to be afraid.

The warrior reached down and touched a spot of red earth paint to Omar's cheek, then moved his hand down to Omar's groin, rubbing, massaging puberty into his cosmos. When Omar opened his eyes, he automatically touched his penis and felt the sticky sperm spread about his pubic area. He had looked about him toward the falls. No one but m'kwi, male black bear, looking for fish, but his fingers had touched the spot of paint, still moist on his cheek.

This memory, and the death of Arlen, and his own strained body, carries Omar's mind and spirit into a deep sleep.

VIII

Annie has not closed her eyes to sleep since night before last. She watches the road, listens for signs. It occurs to her to ask Adrian or some of the young men to go look for Omar, but somehow she knows that Omar must return on his own.

Her body smells earthy like damp leaves. The rain had caught her before daylight while she was gathering herbs. She prepares them and stores them in galvanized dish pans for a sunny day. With this done for now, she nervously opens her sewing box. Inside is a red satin shirt, nearly completed. She busies herself, handstitching navy blue, orange, and white ribbons to the back of the shirt. In her mind, she sees Omar dancing and looking proud in his new shirt.

Annie's face becomes more drawn and taut, as her mind studies Omar's absence. She thinks perhaps it is her years. Even the wind itself senses her uneasiness. "This kind of rain is early this year," she thinks to herself.

As she works, she carries thoughts of Omar into the days of her own childhood, recalling her grandmother who had grown on the earth when there were only rumors of white people. Annie's grandmother was a young girl when she and her brothers, sisters, parents, and grandparents, were herded by the military across the Mississippi River into Missouri, to Kansas, and ultimately, Oklahoma. Annie yet hears the tremor in her grandmother's throat, when she thinks of the mining companies wanting to buy the only land left to them.

Annie sets her stitch work aside and stares above her front door that opens to the east. Above the door is a cedar cane attached to a rawhide bundle. Annie gets up, removes the bundle from its resting place. Attached to the bundle . . . a twist of tobacco and seven bear's teeth. The rawhide crumbles at its edges, and is brittle and splitting throughout. "This must be replaced," she thinks. Her duty has been and is the care of this bundle. The first woman, in the Bear Clan, that has ever possessed it, and, "It must be passed on in order for the people to be strong," Annie had been told.

Rain clouds linger into the evening. Annie lights the kerosene lamp, sets it on the table beside her bed. She sews the contents of the bundle into new skin. Her hands are folded over the old pieces of skin ready to take them outside. She stops. Listens, no whippoorwills this evening. Suddenly a fanning of wings like rushing wind. She jumps back, emptying her folded hands as the loud flutter crashes into her screen door. Semyalwa! His talons lock into the screen beating his wings, frantically trying to pull away.

The wound across Windell's face is pussing terribly. Floyd, his bald head covered with a tan cowboy hat, gulps his beer. . . . . as he drives the trio down the dirt road to Annie's house. Ted looks up, from beneath the bill of his cap, to ask, "Windell, we can't hurt that old woman. Just how do you plan on handling this?" Ted sips his beer, seeming to be in some kind of remorseful thought.

"That damned witch and her skid row grandson have cut their own goddamned throats," Windell says aloud damping a red bandana to his wound. "Don't you guys start gettin' chicken shit on me now. Those coalmine attorneys will pay us good for this, and since I'm on those Ind'n rolls, I've got a right to the per capita that this land will bring in coal money. If I'd known in the bar last night who that Omar was we could have saved ourselves a lot of trouble by making sure he was dead, but it's ok this way.

If Old Annie don't listen to me this time, then the law is going to think Omar came home in a drunken frenzy, set fire to the house, and burned up his old grandmother. With her out of the way, most of the other members are apt to cooperate with the attorneys."

"What about her grandson, that Omar? I know he's on the watch for us . . . in fact, I kinda get the shivers thinking he's out there in these woods watching us," Ted remarks, in second thoughts.

"Don't worry your ass off about Omar. He's probably as rattled as you are, worrying about the cops, or if we're out looking for him somewhere. That's why I brought my shotgun. Loaded her with deer slugs. Blow a hole through that boy as big as Texas. I found this pistol laying on the floorboard of some farmer's truck outside the bar one night last week. Tell the state boys that we got worried about that ole lady out here alone with that *violent* grandson of hers on the rampage, and if we can't talk sense with her, then it's fire. Tell the boys that we saw the flames, and Omar out there holding a pistol saw us coming up and started shooting at us, so we just shot back in self-defense . . . you guys keep this story straight. There's Annie's house right up there. Stop right here, Floyd. Turn your key off. And the lights." Windell steps out of the truck, shotgun in hand, and pistol in his belt.

Annie peers through the willows near the branch . . . watching the movement of headlights. It could be Adrian or someone bringing Omar home, but they would not turn off the motor and lights before coming up to the house. She hears the car doors open, low mumbling through the humid distance. It is Windell, and she knows it. Semyalwa had warned her. Annie breaks from the willows and runs toward the house. For a brief moment she stands outside the window, looking inside to the kerosene glow. It seems as if she can smell the scent of black oak as if it were winter with white smoke billowing out of her chimney across a frozen sky. It is the earth to which she belongs . . . her hair, the rainbow bending into the river. She hears the water drums, sees the faces of her relatives in the firelight, hears the laughter inside the log house that her grandfather and uncles had built. But now she must run. Grabbing up the medicine bundle, the trail to White Bird Creek.

Floyd sees Annie by the light of her window. "Windell, she's seen us! She's running toward the woods!"

"Well, go after her, you sonofabitch!" Windell leaps up on the porch looks inside the window, and enters the house. For an instant, he is caught up in the familiar smell of an Indian house. He hesitates, gazes about the room to the wall of dry herbs, to the beaded eagle's plume hanging above the door, to the fireplace mantle lined with photographs of many children, and pictures taken at powows and feasts. Windell's eyes scan the line of faces, stopping at Omar's 8×10 high school picture. Stuck inside the corner is a picture of a woman holding a baby, probably Omar and his mother, half the photograph has been cut away with scissors.

"To hell with it," Windell shouts as he lifts the lamp and hurls it to the floor. The flames spread, lighting up the dark anger in Windell's face. Clutching his shotgun, Windell allows the screen door to slam for its last time.

IX

Omar sleeps a dead sleep . . . through the afternoon drizzle . . . secure under the ledge. As the sound of the falls drifts into his ears, his body begins to twitch and roll back and forth. He hears the warm up tempo on a water drum. Faceless dancers in bright ribbon shirts emerge from the falls, dancing as if they were on dry land. Two more figures appear. With faces. One is riding the back of

a gigantic deer with brilliant antlers. The rider seems to
be waving to Omar, inviting him. The other figure comes
from the water, approaches Omar. Omar holds his breath.
He sees that the figure's feet are those of a bear, the face
is from his puberty dream, coming closer until they are
face to face. Omar screams at his own reflection. . . .

His eyes are open. There is no one here but Omar, sweat-
ing and shivering with pain, from hunger, from the loss of
his friend. He must go home. His grandmother will cure
him.

Omar leaves the truck where it is and begins trotting
toward the east, upstream. Coming from the forest, into
the clearing before the big hill, he sees a red glow on the
horizon illuminating the low clouds. "What the hell is
that?" he wonders aloud. A feeling of panic overtakes
him. He runs toward the house. From the hilltop, he sees
the flames lighting up the whole valley. To the north is
the red flashing of police cars coming down the dirt road.
He watches them pass around Floyd's car. "Aughhhhh!"
Omar screams, thinking his nohkohmis is in the flames.
At the moment of his cry, Semyalwa returns his call. The
owl's voice sounds as if it comes from near the creek. His
intuition tells him to follow the sound of Semyalwa. In the
light of the fire, Omar runs down the hill, across the
meadow, for the woods that border White Bird Creek.
The lieutenant sees him. Like hounds, they follow.

At the bank of the rising creek Annie looks east where
lightning is still snapping above the mountains. She knows
she must cross this water. Windell and his partners are
crashing through the brush behind her. She runs up
stream to where formerly one could cross atop the boul-
ders. She wedges the medicine bundle into the fork of a
cottonwood. She does not want to chance losing it in the
water. She wades in feeling for the appropriate boulders
by instinct. Her braids have nearly unraveled in the flight,

her long dress balloons up in the cold water. The water is so swift, she nearly loses her balance, but manages to lean herself against the current until she is more than halfway across.

Windell widens his eyes like Semyalwa to detect any movement. He sees her dark form moving near the opposite bank . . . the river just under her breast. Motivated more by images formed in childhood than by greed, Windell knows now that he will not turn back. He calls to her, "Gonawah Hequawi!"

She turns to face him almost within reach of cypress roots.

"You goddamned witch. You could have told me. You could have helped me understand. . . . ." Windell shouts across the water to Annie. The lightning to the east seems to intensify the volume of Windell's voice. "But, no, you gotta hold on to those goddamn Ind'n principles like they was the last gospel. Take that with you on your way to the spirit world."

As Windell lifts the barrel of his gun, Annie shouts, "P'quay manido nela mimitoma p'yatah hojapeke yomi heqwawi!" Windell pulls the trigger. The deafening sound rings in his ears. She crosses her hands high above her body as the slug tears apart the wrinkled skin of her face. Windell is uncertain. He stands yet holding his gun in position. Her body drifts in the rushing silence.

Windell's two cohorts come behind him, but say nothing. Windell wades into the water. Annie's body appears to be snagged in the willows. Holding the gun high above his head with one hand, he balances himself with the other as he crosses the creek . . . exactly where Annie had entered. He must see for himself . . . to touch her body, to be assured that she is at last finished. Ted and Floyd stare at one another, uncertain whether or not to follow or take off into the woods. They hesitate to call out to Windell.

Omar hears the shot echo through the swampy bottoms. It is not the correct sound of thunder. He knows it is a gun. Near the bank, he sees Windell's silhouette moving upstream. Omar removes his shoes and dives into the current, fast stroking and gliding himself to the opposite bank. Not stopping to recover his exhausted breath, he begins running in Windell's direction.

Ted and Floyd hear the cops behind them. They decide quickly that they are unable to explain anything. They call quickly to Windell, who does not answer, even if he hears them. They move rapidly to follow Windell across the river.

At the sound of Ted's voice, Omar stops abruptly to listen for any sound that Windell might make. Omar feels the vibration in his feet . . . in the earth . . . that begins to rumble and quaver violently. Omar braces himself on the gnarled roots of a cypress. Lightning detonates ferociously into the hills upstream. Windell, electrified by the earth's quaking, plummets to the ground near the willows.

Ted and Floyd, midway in the creek, halt to comprehend what is happening. "What the hell is this shaking. This feels like a goddamn earthquake or what?" Floyd's voice breaks like the earth.

"I don't know, Floyd, but let's get the hell out of this water. Windell, come help us get out of here!" Ted's voice falls into silence. The quaking stops. The wind and lightning are without sound.

White Bird Creek, itself, appears to have ceased its moving. Seems like an invisible force is pulling their bodies upstream as if Ted and Floyd are swimming motionless, unable to gain distance to the opposite bank.

Windell stands up. He hears the mystery. And yells, "Get the hell out of there, come on!" Windell lumbers to the water's edge. He hears the roaring upstream. "It's a god-damn flashflood. Come on!"

Tree trunks rip from their banks as the cascading flood thunders down from the hills convulsing over futile screams of Ted and Floyd whose voices are silenced in the violent rage of the storm. Windell stands mesmerized by the flood . . . by the liquid tomb that rampages over the falls and beyond. The creek undulates to a slapping silence except for the bumping of floating logs and limbs.

Windell recovers himself from the trance wondering if the flood has carried away Annie's body as well. He wonders what to do next. He hears the voices of state troopers on the other side of the river. His gun. He remembers leaving it on the ground by where he had fallen. He turns to recover it.

"Don't move. Don't run. Don't do anything. I intend to kill you, Windell Osborne if you cannot tell me where my grandmother is. Where is she?" Windell's face is horror-stricken staring point blank into the barrel of his own murder weapon.

A cool breeze relieves the musky humidity of the late summer storm. Light appears behind the grey veil of clouds that are beginning to dissipate. The last full moon of summer edges its way into gaps of clear sky.

"Omar Little Light," Windell says in a vocal recognition. Windell stares at Omars disfigured face. Omar stares back straining to keep his swollen eyes open.

"Where is Gonawah Hequawi? I will not ask you again."

"Omar, you can buy a lot of booze and good times with the money from the stripmines. They'll pay us plenty. Come on, brother, let's not make this a Cain and Abel incident. Your grandma's alright. She's out here in the woods somewhere hiding."

"I don't believe you, and I am not your brother.

"Well, call for her then. She'll recognize your voice, and come right up here to tell you she's alright."

Omar hesitates, breaks his dead stare from Windell's eyes. He calls, "Nohkohmis . . . Nohkohmis . . . are you there? Nohkohmis! If you can hear me come on over here. It's alright!" There is a cracking of limbs in the willows. Omar turns to the sound.

Windell lunges carrying Omar off the ledge onto the muddy bank. Windell tries to wrest the gun from Omar's grip. Omar explodes his fist into Windell's face. Windell drives his back into Omar. Grappling, struggling for breath, layered with red mud, undistinguishable from the blood that flows. Windell positions himself to jump, slides the gun from Omar's muddied grip but falls back again releasing the gun into White Bird Creek. With his legs, Omar grips Windell about the neck, tightening. Windell gasps for air: "Youu. . . . sum . . bitch . . get . . . de . . uhnn. . . . ."

Windell's fingers search frantically at his beltline for the pistol that he has almost forgotten. His fingers tighten over the butt of the long nosed 38. Plunges the steel barrel into Omar's ribs and pulls the trigger. Omar tightens harder until Windell's face is blue, but Windell fires again, and again until the air rushes back into his lungs. Omar tries to sit up, to brace himself in the mud, stooping forward, glaring into Windell's face. . . .

"I told you, you bastard, that your nohkohmis was waiting on you. Go and see her!" Windell jabs the gun point to Omar's forehead. Omar does not waver, but hears the sounds of hooves, sees the deer coming across the meadow in the moonlight, coming closer, but browsing as they approach as if there is no hurry. Omar does not hear the final blast of the 38.

Windell stands up exhausted but triumphant. It's over. At long last, it's over. He hears the troopers shouting on the other bank apparently frustrated at their fear of crossing the high water. Windell stares momentarily at the sky, the moonlight passes into shadows then to full moonlight again causing Windell's face to appear grotesque from the beating that Omar had given him and the cut across his face that is bleeding again. Windell paces idly, slowly, attempts loosening the mud caked to his curly hair, stops, reflects several times from Omar's body to across the creek.

That crashing in the willows. "What the hell is that? Windell asks himself. He turns to investigate. The massive black shadow clamors from the willows, rises on hind legs. Windell cannot run. The glowing eyes and hot breath of P'quay condensates on Windell's face as steel-like claws furrow through the flesh of his back. The face of P'quay that once appeared gentle, bellows in vengeful fury. Windell cannot move or breath in. He gasps out, "Ahhhhnngh . . . . Goh . . Gonawah . . Hequawi . . . ," as white teeth rip holes for the emission of vomit and dark blood. Windell's body plops to the ground, almost limp. His head, his shoulders jerk in spasmodic contractions in the mud of White Bird Creek.

A bare hint of light appears in clear skies over the hills. Night is yet in the hollows and whippoorwills sing loudly before light takes away their magic. The state police are crossing the creek holding on to a rope tied to trees on opposite banks.

As the first sun breaks into the valley, Adrian, Wanda, their family, and other members gather about the smoking ruins of Annie's house. Younger ones ask, "Where is Nohkohmis? And Omar?"

Mother's clap their hands to silence their children. There are things here that must be felt, not spoken. Adrian,

Wanda, and other male and female elders walk toward the creek where the state police and local deputies congregate near the willows on the opposite side. The police and deputies, walking around like crows in a cornfield, are too busy to notice the assembly of people on the other bank.

Adrian and Wanda's grandson, the one who is always whining, runs from his grandfather's hand, shouting, "P'quay . . P'quay!"

Adrian sees the giant female bear, upstream, rubbing her rear against a cottonwood. Adrian yells, "Naquisah, stop!"

The young grandson stops, cups his hands to his mouth. His brown eyes widen, as P'quay rises threateningly on her rear legs, her cumbersome body collides into the limb above her where the medicine bundle is cradled. The bundle plops to the ground to the left of P'quay. She resettles herself on all fours distracted by the bundle. She sniffs it, nudges it with her nose.

The young child asks, "Methoshena, what is it? What's wrong with P'quay?"

"Hold on, miyon ne lahne, she has had cubs somewhere. It has been a long time for her. You must be careful. Stay away from the creek until the cubs are older," Adrian admonishes his grandson.

"Methoshena, P'quay will not hurt me." The grandson walks reverently toward the bear. P'quay watches him and waits. The grandson stands over the bundle near the breath of P'quay. He stoops, retrieves the bundle. P'quay turns, leaves to attend to her late summer cubs somewhere up on the hillside. The child turns to face his grandfather and walks thoughtfully toward him carrying the bundle in his extended hands.

Adrian, Wanda, and some of the elders gather about the child. A solemnness comes over the crowd. Faces stare at one another then at the child and the bundle. Adrian takes up the bundle, turns to the people, and says, "Autumn will come early this year. It is time for the Green Corn. We all have a lot to do."

The grandson walks patiently beside his grandfather among the people back to their trucks.

Blanket stripes   like
southwest mesa strata
shift my feet beneath to
touch your imaginary leg
i here alone   scratch the
hair on my chest   thinking
when it was good in Santa Fe
high dry air   smelling of
juniper
i played flute this night
in my heart   trying not
to listen to my own song   to
feel the breathing holes
tips of my fingers   i am
strong now   can move more
slowly   like i play the
flute
Creator   daub our bodies
paint us with holy streaks
paint us until we are
chameleons   invisible
against the summer storm.

i said i would see you at
the next dance
somewhere
Faces with big lips
clouded visions in fire
that heat the rocks   Eyes
veiled in dancing heat
stare through years   making
holes in my chest   because
we were too shy to know   to
consummate what almost
began
Wintered in   here in the
northeast   i can see your
pointed shoes   quizzical
face   grooming its reflection
in back street windows of
Rapid City
Once   buffalo herds
thundered in your sleep and
in eyes awed by dreams
To hear your northern voice
      Jeez   in the well of
your throat   i told you
innocent lies   cause i
wanted to breathe your wind
If by thinking of you i
come into your sleep   know
that Santa Fe Indian School
has produced more than one
broken heart
Maybe at the next dance
aieeeeeeeee. . . . .

Stars freeze in midnight mud
on mountain road   crossing
the moonlight
Kerosene lamps faintly glow
in log house windows funneling
out of sight
Inside the truck   heater fan
humms   circulating stale
tobacco air   Silent forms
glued to imitation leather
hear no sounds from Greedy
Ones world
Going into blue dream   each
spirit silhouetted by the
moon   dreams of what the
world will be like
These spirits   wrapped in
winter robes   journey in
on horseback   to warm camps
along the creek   among all
their relatives   to think
about this dream.

Four Wind Vision: Winter Comes From Keshena
for Margaret Richmond
1921–1982

Four winds somersault each
side   over the roof as if
no season existed   coming
through boards as if there
were no walls
Clouds   white   grey to
ominous blue   ration sunlight
rain   snow   on muddy
Algonquin earth   deceiving
those of us accustomed to
winter
Always Watching Hawk carries
my birth blood on his tail
Mirrored spirit glides
inside my eyes   turns his
head   into the snowy owl
My voice shivers over long
wires where P'quay speaks
on the other end
Wind is Indian wind   spirits
as ancient as our creators
voice
i stand in the rainy night
smoking   numbed from what i
did not yet know   but called
it   blood
Night with windows open
kin wind seeps into my
dream marrow   She must
have sat beside me
Morning   vision unfolds
My hand is held high   to
honor the hawk once more as

he dives from mid forest into
sky
Four winds suspend our heart
beats   paint hawk onto
skys grey wall
Her daughters voice on the
long wires   Mom gave up her
breath into the wind last night
Around me   the winds meld
Winter comes all over my skin.

With each death   a
change of tradition
Within my ears   buckskin
to cloth   kerosene lamps to
nuclear bombs   truth to
lies   and my grandparents
whose births led from
oakwood smoke   Ohio River
fog   left me with the
liquid drum   died with
the source in their
hearts.

Grey down   from winter hanging
too long over planting time
Stories   winter time for
telling   staying   until my
dream realities outweigh
daylight
She was here   again   not at
home   but a familiar
dream hill   the tallest
cedar tree   a sagegrass
ball   She lay inside
dying   Two nights i
was by her   felt her
grandmother blood all over me
until the rain   night and day
soaking the sacred hill   blue
mist rising   White plumed spirit
turned to flesh   descended from
the tree   said it was
dry inside   Go back   smell
for the last time   chrysalis
image
Cedar power   this ancient
homeland spirit soaked into
my hands   grasping tightly
each limb   until i climbed in
beside her
At last it was spring   where
she tended her flowers   her
blackberry fields   and
grandfather shouted at the
horses.

Sleet pelts hard on the
tracks   hard trailing
if careless eyes miss the
blood   and stumbling
Bad spirits are bold
sometimes rash   concealed
like in Aladdins lamp
waiting for the hearts thumb
to caress the side of
the bottle
But these bold eyes
caress faces of my people
say silently as we drink
and eat their drugs   the
more we become like them
enemies even to ourselves
We are the gladiators
while world governments
applaud   unconcerned for
humanity   except for the
gold teeth they extract
Brown sage grass crunches
under feet   sleet to
rain   tracking almost
impossible
What the enemy doesnt
know   strong hearts and
clear heads call allies
in harmony with each
change of wind
Snow melts to mud
With confident eyes   draw
the arrows
In the thicket   hear the
wounded one   panting.

Moons Last Round
this song for lance henson

Moons last round before
ice   fragile cicles
hang in the breath of
your cheyenne voice
Last utterance is
soundless like this moon
this moon where semyalwa
rides on your shoulder
makes words for the last
song   the one that
we both hear
And when this song is
ready   we will hear
it coming from each
others eyes   nod
pull on our moccasins   go
into this night of
blankets   and
take our places

She begins her Havad talk
LA flight to Boston   her
arms folded   legs crossed
A frightened american who
must be drunk to talk   opens
to a stranger who appears
like iron
Computer tape breaks   human
voices fall to earth
She loves animals   and
children   but fears all
else
She unfolds when words lead
to death   end of this brief
encounter   brief words on
a plane
Mimitoma   Strange   what
americans fear   The word
is prayer   to set ones
feet in balance on this
road
Her concrete eyes soften like
a young childs   weeps
90 proof
In Boston airport   we walk
like childhood friends   even
though her skiis have gone
to Guadalajara   and
my friend has not come to
meet me
We wait in airport lounge
Drinks are ordered
Two more   Boston drinks
at three and nine dollars
a whack   im thinking of
Guadalajara too
Steve   my friend   suddenly

arrives   wondering what
road we are on tonight
We all embrace   promise to
call   departing into
Bostons coldest winter
ever.

In the Pittsburg airport
changing planes from
Minneapolis   i have no
braids   wear no water
bird earrings hanging to
my chest   no ribbon shirt
no choker   moccasins or
cowboy boots   but old
leather tennis shoes this
time   and a beaded
belt buckle under the
fold of my shirt   Still
this business suited white
man unnerves me with his
stare   i look around to
other eyes watching   not
even looking away as i
note them
My first voice says   Be
Strong   It is the
Medewin drum yet pounding
inside   voices   songs
in one hundred thousand
years   a brief time in
the ring of eternity.

Passing boyhood into a
combination of numbers
created by seasons and
europes outline for
adulthood   i yet live
inside the skin of
freedom   see highways
to Colorado flashing
underneath the vehicle
in my head   cross with
moccasined feet into
my relatives arena
dance all night until
our dioxin infected
blood is cleansed
Winter yet rages across
americas calendars
declaring spring   yet
winter is deaf to the
will of ordered society
      laugh   not because
the greedyones
weaknesses are bared
which are for pity
i laugh because winter
is one of the directions
that created
human beings.

Lake Michigan Revisited at 6AM

Late winter   Lake Michigan
Winters last blue overcast
lingers   to
waterblades sharp horizon
Waves roll in   lusterless green
slowly   like a spirit awakening
from winters long sleep
stretching and yawning
Old 49 spots   old visions
that were new when i first was
in their dreams   ten years past
and our southern songs   blended
with northern drumming on car
hoods   i know now   anyplace
can be holy   With his flute
Comanche Ed enticed the water
to come closer   until waves
baptized the dawn   baptized my
hearts slurred voice   on
countless nights that i have
stood beside this water   stirring
that ones Chippewa spirit into
a new galvanic chaos   loving
it   my own riotuous blood   the
dawn   the twelve packs   the
promises   the laughter   and
being a hundred thousand year old
warrior on Milwaukees wet edge.

Wrapped in
blanket   in
tobacco smoke from
my pipe   i am here
somewhere like a ghost
a phrase from a history
text   sitting at the
window   eyes crossing hills
looking for relatives
relatives who know
that we are the
way of this
land   Whites
know it too   wanting
an identity but cannot
find in this land what was
left in europe   but yet they
search   stripping and tearing at
the earth   devastating native
lives in whose eyes yet lurk
the seven cities of Cibola
They see us but cannot
hear   They read
that we stood
and fought
endured
all the genocide
bullshit   for homes
families   survival and
they know cowardice   how
they fled europe   becoming
traitors   using freedom and
religion as passports   but it
is greed that all this dying has
been about   Strange you white
man   what you die for   strange lies
you tell your children   They

would know truth if your
hearts were in this
land   There is
always truth
at the
source.

Warm fire   images
go into beadwork
its smokey odor on
buckskin for moccasins
Winter coming wind is
sinew for stitching
soles   to fit
snugly your brown
feet.

About the Author

In his near forty years, Barney Bush has traveled North America by foot and thumb, by car, bus, train, airplane, and by raft and canoe. Born into a family of hunters and trappers, whose ancestoral homelands lay on both sides of the Ohio River, he has relatives from Southern Illinois through Eastern Oklahoma and beyond.

"Like our ancestors who traveled and visited from ocean to ocean for thousands of years before European Colonialism, many of us continue our journeys over this sacred earth—often mixing blood with other tribes and sometimes with foreigners. My eyes have logged brutal sights and needless bloodshed, as well as beauty that lights my road with purposeful steps. . . . but it is the journey, and the desire for freedom. To live in the manner that Colonial America establishes around the world is death, no matter its "good intentions," or its terminology. All of Creation's survivors see it, hear it, smell it, taste it, feel it, and dread it. Civilization has become the most vulgar of its words."

Barney began writing professionally in the early seventies while yet an undergraduate student at Ft. Lewis College in Durango, Colorado. He gave his first reading at the 1971 Southwest Poet's Conference at Many Farms, Arizona, in the Navajo Nation. Since then, he has given readings and workshops throughout North America, often with flute accompaniment by Comanche musician, Ed

Wapp, Jr. Barney's poetry has also appeared in dozens of anthologies, journals, magazines, and other publications here and in Europe. His poetry has been translated into French, Macedonian, Serbian, Yugoslavian, Spanish, and Frisian, an ancient language still spoken in the Netherlands. INHERIT THE BLOOD is his fourth book.

After completing a Master's Degree in English and Fine Arts at the University of Idaho, Moscow, 1980, Bush was awarded a writer's grant from National Endowment for the Arts. He has served as Writer-in-Residence in Oklahoma, Illinois, Kentucky, New York, Vermont, and is presently, Visiting Writer for the state of North Carolina. Currently, he and his sixteen year old son, Phil, live in the northwoods of Vermont near the Canadian border.

About the Artist

Daryl Trivieri is Oneida with Italian and other ancestry. Born in early January, 1957, New York state, Daryl says, "When I was a child growing up in this world, I realized two important traits in my life: one, being interested in drawing what I saw and felt; second, being awed by life and all its strange behaviors."

Although Daryl received the major portion of his education from the University of Self Taught, he has also attended the Munson Williams Proctor Institute of Art. Recent exhibitions include: "New Realist," Cote' Galleries, Huntington, NY, 1982
"New Realist," Cote' Galleries, Rockvill Centre, NY, 1982
"Three Former Students," Munson Williams Proctor Institute, 1983
"Surrealist Art Exhibition," Fort Schuyler Gallery, 1983

In addition to his art, Daryl also writes. A recent story entitled, "Petroglyphs," appeared in the August 1984 issue of "Heavy Metal Magazine." Daryl is also cited in, "Air Brushing in America, Volume I," published by Von Nostrand Rienhold, Inc., 1984. He presently resides in Utica, New York with Patricia and a menage of wildlife.

Other Books by Thunder's Mouth Press

The Red Menace, Michael Anania

Coagulations: New and Selected Poems, Jayne Cortez

To Those Who Have Gone Home Tired, W.D. Ehrhart

She Had Some Horses, Joy Harjo

Dos Indios, Harold Jaffe

Living Room, June Jordan

America Made Me, Hans Koning

When the Revolution Really, Peter Michelson

Echoes Inside the Labyrinth, Thomas McGrath

Fightin', Simon J. Ortiz

From Sand Creek, Simon J. Ortiz

Saturday Night at San Marcos, William Packard

The Mojo Hands Call/I Must Go, Sterling Plumpp

Somehow We Survive, Sterling Plumpp

Homegirls and Handgrenades, Sonia Sanchez

The Man Who Cried I Am, John A. Williams